THE
GRANDPARENT
BOOK

THE GRANDPARENT BOOK

LINDA B. WHITE, MD

Illustrations by Diane Waller

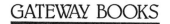

GATEWAY BOOKS

San Francisco

Gateway Books
San Francisco

Library of Congress Cataloging-in-Publication Data

White, Linda B. (Linda Blachly)
   The grandparent book : an entertaining and informative guide / by Linda B. White
      p. cm.
   Includes bibligraphical references.
   ISBN 0-933469-07-1 : $11.95
   1. Grandparenting—United States.   I. Title
HQ759.9.W47 1989
306.874'5—dc20   89-23730
                                                                              CIP

10 9 8 7 6 5 4 3 2 1

Acknowledgements

Special thanks to Nancy White Lippe, Barney White, and Patricia Hass for making this book possible.

Thanks to Alexander and Darcy White for making me a link in the chain.

Thanks to Barbara, Catherine, Melissa, Amy, and Kerstin for playing with Alex and Darcy while I wrote.

Thanks to Debby Faes, C.H.A., Barbara Hughes, C.N.M., John E. Johnson, M.D., Mary Kohn, M.D., Susan Moison, M.D., Marianne Neifert, M.D., Barton Schmitt, M.D., and Bill Sykes, M.D. for their assistance.

Contents

Dedicated to

Lorraine and Ross
and
Marion and Byron

Introduction

Welcome to grandparenthood, a magical realm that carries with it many advantages noticeably absent from the more practical, earth-bound realm of parenthood. Unless you are a grandparent who acts as a surrogate parent to your grandchildren, you can now step out of the role of authoritarian police person and sergeant-at-arms and into the far more pleasurable guise of court magician. To your grandchildren, you are that special person who offers uncritical friendship and unconditional love. Because you are not the poor parent caught up in trying to mold a small creature into a socially acceptable human being, your relationship with your grandchild is remarkably free of the tension that normally sneaks into the parent-child relationship.

You, like many other grandparents, might find that you enjoy your grandchildren more than you did your own children. Having raised your own brood, you already know how children work and so can fall into a more relaxed style with your grandchildren. Hindsight has taught you that many things that worried you about your own children's behavior mattered little in the long run. For instance, your six-foot-tall son writes bestselling novels despite the fact that he still won't eat his lima beans.

Becoming a grandparent is often invigorating. If your life has become less cluttered with domestic and professional distractions, you can give your grandchildren your complete attention when you visit. Children know when an adult is only half listening and will adore you for making them feel special.

And because grandparents usually are not with their grandchildren all the time, you bring to them a refreshing enthusiasm. Gone are the days of seemingly relentless child care inherent in parenthood. As a venerable grandparent, you can set your own limits for babysitting detail. You can play with your marvelous progeny to your heart's content and then withdraw to your own peace and quiet.

With the arrival of the youngest generation comes a sense of continuity. Your magnificent genes are on their way to immortality. Each of your grandchildren will inherit one quarter of your genes. When you look into a grandchild's face you may see mirrored back your red hair, a mischievous twinkle in a blue eye, a wry smile divulging a playful sense of humor—gifts from Grandma or Grandpa.

Your elevation to the status of grandparent can also make you uncomfortably mindful of your own mortality. You may

now have the dubious distinction of being a member of the oldest generation—a veritable fossil.

But before you start obsessing on wrinkles, white hairs, and stiff joints, consider some of the positive ways grandparenthood has changed. Because people are living longer, you modern grandparents stand to benefit by being around long enough to get to know your grandchildren. And because people are having fewer children, you have fewer grandchildren to compete for your attention. You are also blessed with earlier retirement, greater wealth, and more leisure time than grandparents of generations past. In other words, you can derive more enjoyment from and lavish more of your attention on each grandchild, thereby creating a lasting impression on your progeny.

Grandchildren can also bring you closer to their parents, your adult children. After spending countless years in prolonged adolescence when your children rejected your values and "couldn't relate" to you, the dawn of parenthood miraculously infuses these ingrates with new insight and understanding into your experiences as parents. You now share parenthood as a common bond. Your children will take sudden interest in stories about the silly and exasperating things they did as small children. In exchange, you will get earfulls of their parenting adventures. Yours is the satisfaction of knowing that your children will come to appreciate from first-hand experience both the ecstasy and the occasional misery they once caused you.

Just as grandchildren can act like warm, cuddly glue bonding you and your children, the youngest generation can also introduce new tensions into your relationship with your children. Some of the conflicts between parents and grandparents stem from misunderstanding. Although babies haven't changed, obstetrics and pediatrics have undergone a metamorphosis over the last few decades, creating a potential generation gap between new parents and grandparents.

The main objective of *The Grandparent Book* is to narrow this generation gap by bringing you up to date on the ways childbirth and child-rearing philosophies have changed since you had your babies. If you understand the rationale behind your children's foreign ideas, you may be able to at least tolerate their seemingly odd behavior. And because parents are usually the gatekeepers to your grandchildren, diplomacy is your passport to delight.

The Grandparent Book does not presume to tell you how to be a grandparent. You know instinctively how to love your grandchildren. You know from experience how to care for them. Furthermore, books have already been written that provide tips about fun activities for grandparents and grandchildren to share. Neither does this book delve deeply into intergenerational relationships. Psychiatrists and psychologists have authored books to help grandparents maximize rapport with their children and grandchildren.

I have enjoyed writing this book and hope you enjoy reading it. As a physician with specialized training in pediatrics, a free-lance writer for parenting magazines and books, and a mother of two delightful children blessed with loving grandparents, I found writing a book for grandparents about trends in childbirth and child rearing to be a natural extension of my work.

So what exactly does *The Grandparent Book* have that could possibly interest you, an expert on children in your own right?

☐ The first chapter discusses pregnancy. Conception, which used to take place largely in bedrooms and automobiles, now also occurs in scientific laboratories. (This has nothing to do with kinky sexual habits.)

☐ The second chapter talks about changes in prenatal care, including a brief explanation of modern diagnostic tests—so that you don't sound like Rip Van Winkle when talking to the expectant parents.

☐ The third chapter is designed to help you mentally prepare yourself for grandparenthood by asking yourself some important questions, such as "Do I like babies?" It also gives you pointers on how you can help the expectant parents.

☐ The fourth chapter provides a historical overview of childbirth practices. You learn astonishing facts, such as that women are no longer routinely put to sleep during the birth. Not only mothers, but fathers, too, can actively participate in the birth of their children. Men are no longer at liberty merely to pace the waiting-room floor.

☐ Chapter five briefs you on who is likely to deliver the baby and where—so that you are not unduly shocked by either a home birth with a midwife or a high-tech hospital birth.

☐ The sixth chapter discusses changes in hospital routine, such as babies (and fathers) rooming-in with mothers and shrinking hospital stays. This chapter also discusses the specific needs of each family member and how you as a grandparent can help make yourself and others comfortable.

☐ And because close relationships are not without their friction points, Chapter seven provides you with a list of ways you and the parents can drive each other crazy and offers simple suggestions for dealing with each pitfall.

☐ Chapter eight is an aside on changing roles for mothers, fathers, and grandparents—complete with editorial comments on the relative forward or backward progress achieved.

☐ The next two chapters are provided as brief reviews of infant growth and development and of basic baby care. If you already know at what age a baby has fully functional vision and hearing; if you already know what the startle reflex is; if you already know when your grandchild is likely to sit; if you still remember all the reasons babies cry and what maneuvers are comforting—then you should skip these chapters.

☐ Chapter eleven deals with changing feeding philosophies. If you believe most women don't have enough breast milk and should supplement with formula and that babies should be fed cereal by the second week of life, please read this chapter.

☐ Chapter twelve answers questions about shifting child-rearing philosophies. How old does your grandbaby have to be before it is possible to spoil him? Should anyone ever strike your grandchild? What is the best way to discipline your young grandchild? Do pacifiers deform teeth and moral character? Why do toddlers

15

have temper tantrums and what can you do when Junior has one in the grocery store? When are the parents ever going to potty train your grandchild?

☐ The last chapter prepares you for a visit with your grandchildren, includes lists of things to have on hand if they are coming to your place, and offers guidelines for what to do should a grandchild fall ill under your care.

Throughout the book, I refer to the mother of your grandchild as "your daughter," to the father as "your son," and to the parents as "your children." Although I realize that at least one of the parents is an in-law, the phrases "daughter or daughter-in-law" and "son or son-in-law" seem too cumbersome. Also, rather than writing "he or she" or "she/he," I randomly interchange these pronouns when talking about your grandchild.

Chapter One

A GRANDCHILD IS CONCEIVED

And Hence, a Grandparent

If your children have conceived a grandbaby for you, congratulations! People generally have less control about becoming grandparents than they do about becoming parents.

But now that you're actually on your way to becoming a grandparent, why not move on to a discussion of what you can buy, make, or borrow for your future grandbaby? Why should a grandparent read a chapter on pregnancy? How could something so basic change?

A young couple makes love and conceives a baby. Then, they wait around for nine months as the mother's girth increases— perhaps doing things like periodically checking in with the doctor and fixing up a nursery. Not much to it, right?

Well, yes and no. Obstetrical technology has advanced. On the one hand, it can gallantly rescue some couples who not long ago would have been labeled barren. On the other hand, it presents even healthy pregnant women with a barrage of diagnostic tests. This chapter briefly reviews the physiology of pregnancy and explains commonly used obstetrical terminology.

Today's expectant parents are more aggressive about learning about pregnancy. This review will help keep you on a par with their knowledge. And because your adult children may

have had to overcome obstacles to fertility, new-fangled ways of conceiving are outlined. The subsequent chapter talks about prenatal care and the gamut of available prenatal diagnostic tests.

How Does Pregnancy Occur?

At your stage in life, an explanation of the birds and the bees is probably unnecessary. You know that the answer to the question "Where do babies come from?" is not "The stork."

Let's contrast the time-honored method of making a baby with some of the high-tech variations currently in practice. The old-fashioned way of procreating is to "make love" to a consenting adult of the opposite sex. If the time is right, a rather unscrupulous sperm encounters an unsuspecting egg within one of the woman's Fallopian tubes. The sperm penetrates the modest egg's defenses and, presto, fertilization occurs.

The fertilized egg, or zygote, begins dividing and travels down the Fallopian tube into the uterus, or womb, where it burrows into the spongy uterine walls. Some of the dividing cells become the *embryo*, which later is called a *fetus* until birth (at which time he can correctly be called a baby). Other embryonic cells contribute to the *placenta*, the organ that unites the developing fetus and the mother.

Now, thanks to modern technology, the events leading up to the miracle of life are far more creative. What has spurred the development of these innovations?

As you may know, not everyone can have babies. For instance, despite the illusions created by cosmetics and plastic surgery, some people are too old. On the other extreme, despite the liberal use of makeup, other people are too young. Other folks are smack dab in their reproductive years, yet, despite ideal circumstances (such as a mate of the opposite sex), they cannot make a baby.

What causes infertility? Without getting too technical, let's just say that the problem may lie with the man (insufficient numbers of normal sperm) or with the woman (hormonal irregularities, mechanical problems with the reproductive organs, etc.).

What does Science have to offer these young hopefuls? First of all, a vigorous *infertility workup*. In your day, couples who couldn't make a baby eventually got used to the idea and perhaps adopted one. Instead, modern couples can now answer many probing and intimate questions posed by a physician in a white laboratory coat.

After the doctor has established that there is indeed a problem (the woman is not pregnant after 12 months of regular sexual intercourse without birth control), the couple can submit to a thorough physical exam and a variety of tests. Levels of sex hormones are measured, egg and sperm production are monitored, and the various tubes of the reproductive system are examined for defects.

Then what? Depending on the results of the tests, several remedies are available. For example, if a man has low levels of testosterone, he can take hormones to stimulate sperm production. If a woman is not producing eggs (ovulating) properly, she can take "fertility drugs" and run the slight risk of delivering a litter.

Failing the usual corrective measures to induce pregnancy, a couple (who meet certain criteria) can attempt more inventive means of making a baby. Putting a bun in the oven just isn't as simple and straightforward as it used to be. On the other hand, some young couples, who in earlier generations would have resigned themselves to barrenness, can create new life.

Nontraditional Ways of Making a Baby

1. **Artificial Insemination.** In this case, the woman is fertile, but the man is infertile. This woman can be *artificially inseminated* with another man's sperm. Adultery is not involved. Rather, within the sterile confines of an examining room, a fully clothed physician instills precollected sperm into the woman's vagina with an instrument resembling a turkey baster.

2. **Gamete Intra-Fallopian Transfer or GIFT.** Although unable to conceive a child, the man is fertile and the woman possesses at least one Fallopian tube that opens normally into the womb. The woman is "primed" with hormones to induce a bountiful crop of ova (eggs), that are then "harvested" by the physician. Meanwhile, the man has donated some of his precious sperm. The sperm and eggs are then simultaneously squirted into the woman's Fallopian tube. Ideally, fertilization takes place here, which is where it occurs normally. From this point on, the dance of life follows the usual steps.

3. **In Vitro Fertilization or IVF.** "In vitro" means outside the living body. More specifically, IVF refers to a process whereby the woman's ova and the man's sperm are united in a sterile laboratory dish. The fertilized eggs are transferred to the woman's uterus where, hopefully, at least one grows to be a baby.

4. **Surrogate Mothers.** If a husband is fertile, but his wife isn't, the couple may decide to hire a woman to be artificially inseminated with the husband's sperm and carry the baby to term. The agreement is that the surrogate mother will relinquish the baby to said couple at birth. If you follow the news, you are aware that the surrogate mom may *bond* with the baby and refuse to give it up. (Bonding has nothing to do with tying up people. See Chapter six.)

After your children successfully conceive your grandbaby, then what happens? As you will recall, during the ensuing long nine months the net result is that both the mother and fetus grow

larger. Both undergo complex anatomic and physiologic changes (which you will be relieved to know will *not* be covered in this book).

Although not without its share of side effects, pregnancy is not a disease. Furthermore, it is not a permanent condition. Most pregnant women lose sight of this latter well-known medical fact as gestation stretches before them like an eternity. One of your jobs as an expectant grandparent is to remind your daughter that pregnancy lasts a finite length of time.

Just how long does this pregnant condition persist? Close scientific scrutiny of the pregnant Homo sapiens has revealed that the average pregnancy lasts roughly nine calendar months or forty weeks. Ninety-eight percent of babies are delivered at *term* or between weeks 37 and 42. Births that occur before this time are called *premature*. Conversely, babies who linger inside the womb longer than 42 weeks are *postmature*.

The pregnancy is divided into three time periods called *trimesters*, each lasting three months, or roughly 13 weeks.

The table on page 24 summarizes the more dramatic changes that take place by trimester.

HELPFUL HINTS

Do reinforce your daughter's self-image as a warm, glowing earth mother. Tell her that the pregnancy becomes her. Do not say, "Just because you resemble a giant turnip on legs, you are not unattractive, dear."

Do remind your daughter that the average pregnancy lasts only 40 weeks. Compare this to the gestation of an elephant (21 months), not of a housecat (9 weeks).

Do not encourage your daughter to "eat for two." Remember that the fetus is not even the size of an orange until the second trimester. She'll not thank you later on if she is still wearing maternity clothes at your grandbaby's first birthday.

Unless she requests otherwise, do not telephone your daughter at frequent intervals during the last trimester. Don't call hourly and ask sweetly, "Has the baby come YET?" You may incite hysteria.

PREGNANCY - Summary of Changes by Trimester

	First Trimester	Second Trimester	Third Trimester
Mother	Looks basicallly the same, but may feel tired, generally lousy, & suffer from nausea, vomiting, heartburn, indigestion, constipation, ambivalence, & weepiness.	Begins to look pregnant. Feels better—except for backache, swelling of hands & feet, varicose veins, hemorrhoids, & weepiness.	Obviously pregnant. Self- inspection below the navel (now an "outie") difficult. Excited, irritable, insomniac (can't sleep face down), restless, & weepy.
Baby	Conception. Major organs formed.	Grows rapidly. Movements now felt by mother.	Further growth & maturation. All sensations (touch, smell, taste, hearing, vision) function.
Father	Sympathy symptoms in some cultures.	Feels ambivalent— excited and anxious. Looks at life insurance. Looks at family-sized cars. Paints nursery.	Feels nervous, eager, excited.
Grandparents	Feel ambivalent—joyful, reminded of age.		Flip through old baby books. Take up knitting.Clean attic of old baby paraphernalia. Feel excited & nervous.

Chapter Two

PRENATAL CARE

Understanding Your Pregnant Daughter

In these days of sophisticated medical technology, how does a woman know for sure she is with child? If a pregnant woman waits long enough, her condition will eventually become obvious to everyone. If she is impatient, as many women are, she can find out very soon indeed.

A big advance in the field of obstetrics is that the lab technician no longer needs a rabbit to diagnose pregnancy. Soon after conception, the tiny embryo manufactures a hormone called *HCG* (short for *human chorionic gonadotrophin*). This hormone can be detected by a simple blood test about ten days after conception, or by an even simpler urine test four days after a missed menstrual period. Your pregnant daughter doesn't even need to visit her doctor to diagnose pregnancy. She can just waltz (in disguise) into her local supermarket or pharmacy and purchase a home urine pregnancy test.

What's the rush? Why find out sooner rather than later? So that she can begin *prenatal care* immediately. Studies have shown that women who are attended by medical professionals throughout pregnancy tend to give birth to healthier babies. Regular checkups allow complications to be diagnosed early and treated promptly.

Surprisingly, prenatal care is a relatively modern invention. Until the twentieth century, a pregnant woman did not seek the assistance of a midwife or physician before the onset of labor, unless a complication arose. Nurses introduced prenatal care by making home visits at the request of a pregnant woman. Eventually, routine prenatal care was recognized as essential to optimizing the health of both mother and baby.

Currently in the United States, the usual schedule of obstetrical exams is as follows: every four weeks until the 32nd week of pregnancy, every two weeks between 32 and 36 weeks, and every week from 36 weeks until the birth.

The First Prenatal Visit

During the first visit the doctor or midwife will want to know about your daughter's general state of health and will ask about her medical history and family history. You expectant grandparents should be sure to inform your children about any hereditary illnesses. Ideally, your children should hear this information *before* planning their families.

Examples of some common inheritable diseases are sickle cell anemia, cystic fibrosis, Tay Sachs disease, and muscular dystrophy. Some diseases, such as diabetes mellitus and high blood pressure, have a tendency to "run in families," but are not due to the inheritance of a single defective gene. The doctor or midwife will want to know if there is a family history of multiple births, mental retardation, or children born with birth defects. No one needs to worry about Uncle Willy's hammer toes, Aunt Matilda's bunions, or Cousin Grace's overbite.

After relaying the medical history, your daughter should receive a complete physical exam and undergo a few routine blood and urine laboratory tests.

Based upon your daughter's menstrual history, physical exam, and the pregnancy test, the doctor or midwife can estimate her *due date*. This date, which is roughly 40 weeks from her last menstrual period, gives an *approximation* of when she will deliver the baby. Normally, the birth will occur within two weeks on either side of this date. You can help your daughter avoid major disappointment by making sure she is not counting on the birth occurring precisely on her due date.

Subsequent Visits

The subsequent visits are much briefer. First, your pregnant daughter has an opportunity to complain about her nausea, hemorrhoids, and low back pain. Then, the doctor or midwife swiftly reassures her that these pregnancy-related symptoms will largely disappear in several months when she delivers the baby.

Next, your daughter lumbers over to the scales to check that she is neither eating for herself and Orson Welles nor trying to prevent the inevitable pregnant bulges by starving herself. She obligingly produces a urine specimen. Her blood pressure is checked. The practitioner pokes and measures your daughter's expanding abdomen to determine the rate of growth, and later, the position of the baby. Using either a modified stethoscope called a fetoscope or an ultrasonic devise called a Doptone, he or she listens to the fetal heart sounds.

It is now more common for an expectant father to accompany the mother on these visits. His show of support can mean a great deal to the mother. It is also important for him to get to know the obstetrician or midwife, because they will be working together during the birth. Furthermore, when a father listens to the fetal heartbeat or observes the fetus during an ultrasound exam, the pregnancy becomes more real for him.

If you are interested and feel that your daughter might appreciate your support, you might ask her whether she'd like you to come with her for a prenatal visit.

Pregnancy—Do's and Don'ts

Much of the advice about how a woman should care for herself during her pregnancy revolves around common sense. For instance, pregnancy is not the time to try out for the local football team nor to enter the Rachel Welch look-alike contest. However, over the last couple of decades, some recommendations have been revised. In case you would like to know about them to better help you understand your daughter's behavior, the major do's and don'ts follow.

Diet: Pregnant women are advised to follow a balanced diet that meets their increased nutritional demands (of roughly 300 extra calories per day). Vitamin supplements are often prescribed.

Weight gain: Expectant mothers are counselled to gain an average of 25 to 30 pounds over the entire pregnancy. You grandmothers may have been advised to gain more or less weight. The understanding now is that either extreme carries attendant risks for both the mother and the baby.

Cigarettes: Pregnant women should not smoke. Smoking is responsible for more than 13,000 deaths in fetuses and newborns each year. During pregnancy, the main risk that smoking causes is impaired blood flow and oxygen delivery to the fetus. The result is an increased incidence of miscarriages, low birth weight babies, and newborn illnesses.

"Passive" smoking (inhaling smokey air generated by another's cigarette) is also damaging to both children and adults. It not only increases the risk of respiratory infections but also has been linked to a growing list of cancers. If you are a smoker, avoid exposing your pregnant daughter or grandchildren (or any other nonsmokers) to smokey air.

Alcohol: Most doctors advise that pregnant women either abstain from alcoholic beverages entirely or limit their consumption to an occasional drink. Drinking alcohol has been associated with an increased risk of miscarriages, low birth weight babies, infant mortality, childhood learning disabilities, and a particular birth defect called the fetal alcohol syndrome. Do your daughter (and your unborn grandchild) a favor by not encouraging her to have a drink.

Caffeine: Pregnant women are urged to switch to decaffinated beverages or limit their intake of tea or coffee to less than two cups a day. Research on the effects of caffeine on the unborn has yielded confusing results, but some studies do show increased fetal death, miscarriages, and stillbirths associated with very high caffeine intake.

Nonprescription drugs: Drugs such as marijuana, narcotics, amphetamines, cocaine, etc., should not be used during pregnancy. Your daughter should consult her physician before taking over-the-counter medications. Even seemingly harmless drugs such as aspirin may have adverse effects when taken during pregnancy.

Prescription drugs: Your daughter should also check with her doctor before continuing any prescription drugs during her pregnancy.

31

Other environmental exposures: Your expectant daughter should avoid exposure to any toxic materials at home or in the workplace. The list of toxic substances is lengthy and includes pesticides, paint thinners, paint and varnish removers, paints containing lead, solvents, strong detergents, radioactive compounds, and X-rays.

Exercise: All people should exercise regularly. Pregnancy should not be used as an excuse to take a break. In fact, *proper* exercise ameliorates some of the side effects of pregnancy, conditions a woman for the birth, and helps to hasten her recuperation after the birth. If your daughter needs encouragement, you can invite her to accompany you on walks. (Some activities are contraindicated during pregnancy. Your daughter should consult her doctor or midwife if she has questions.)

Work outside the home: If your daughter is healthy, she need not quit her job because she is pregnant. Heavy lifting and exposure to toxic substances are prohibited. Obviously, fatigue is a signal your daughter should cut back on her workload. If she is already engaged in the the strenuous task of raising small children (a job she can't quit), your daughter should rest whenever possible.

Travel: If your daughter has had no complications with her pregnancy, she does not have to restrict her travels. Some doctors and midwives request that the expectant mother stay within striking distance of the selected birth place during the last month. Furthermore, flight attendants and hotel clerks may cast a worried glance over the pendulous abdomen of a woman traveling during the third trimester.

Stress: Pregnancy is a time of many changes and places many demands on a woman's body. Therefore, your expectant daughter should take adequate time for rest and relaxation. Expectant fathers and grandparents can help by shouldering some of the domestic duties. You may also be able to alleviate some of her tension by encouraging her to express her feelings about pregnancy and motherhood

Prenatal Diagnostic Tests
Examining the Unborn

Birth holds fewer surprises than it did for previous generations. Over the last two decades, incredible strides have been taken in prenatal diagnosis. The goal of these diagnostic tests is to identify serious abnormalities among the unborn. Sometimes steps can be taken to treat the fetus in the womb. Otherwise, doctors and parents can either prepare themselves to cope with a sick baby after the birth or chose to terminate the pregnancy. Fortunately, however, serious complications of pregnancy are rare and most babies are blessed with good health.

Many prenatal diagnostic tests are used with such frequency that you may have heard of them already. Brief descriptions of the commonly used procedures are included to help you stay abreast of the tide of obstetrical technology.

Quite possibly, you are wondering why women and doctors don't muddle through pregnancy, letting nature take her course. Why all these complicated tests? Bear in mind that some pregnant women manage to sneak through the entire nine months unmolested by obstetrical technology. But the very fact that the technology exists makes it difficult not to use.

For each patient, doctors have to weigh the risks versus the benefits of prenatal diagnosis. Obstetricians are often caught between not wanting to intervene and worrying about their

---

Prenatal Diagnostic Procedures

Ultrasound or echosonography is a painless procedure frequently employed to determine the size and age of the fetus and to detect major defects of organs such as the heart, bones, brain, and spinal cord. It is not a completely accurate method of distinguishing girls from boys.

This test is performed by placing a transducer of high frequency sound waves on the mother's abdomen. As the sound waves bounce back they are converted to images on a TV-like screen. Parents (and grandparents) usually delight in watching the fuzzy outlines of their unborn baby.

Amniocentesis is the most definitive test available for diagnosing serious fetal malformations, chromosomal defects, and a host of hereditary diseases. If they want to want to find out, parents can also learn their baby's sex.

An amniocentesis is usually done between the l4th and l8th weeks of pregnancy. Under local anesthesia, a small needle is passed through the mother's abdominal wall into the fluid-filled space surrounding the fetus. Ultrasound is frequently used to guide the needle. A small amount of this fluid, called amniotic fluid, is withdrawn and sent to a laboratory for analysis. Results are available one or two weeks later.

Amniocentesis is performed when there is a significant risk that something might be wrong with the fetus. A common indication for amniocentesis is "advanced maternal age" (this label starts at 33 or 35). As a woman ages, her chances increase for conceiving a baby with a chromosomal disorder such as Down Syndrome (mongolism). Parents who have previously given birth to a baby with a chromosomal abnormality, genetic disease or birth defect, or who are carriers of a hereditary disease are also encouraged to take advantage of amniocentesis.

Theoretically, amniocentesis is used when the benefit of diagnosing a serious problem in the newborn outweighs the potential risk of the test. The risks of amniocenetesis are injury to the fetus, infection, bleeding and miscarriage. All but the latter are exceedingly rare complications. The risk of causing a miscarriage is less than 1 in 200.

Chorionic villus sampling has recently emerged as a potential alternative to amniocentesis. It is still considered experimental and is not widely available.

This procedure is done by passing a very slender, hollow plastic tube (catheter) through the cervix into the uterus. The doctor uses ultrasound imaging to guide the catheter tip to the placenta. A few of these cells are suctioned into the catheter.

Because the developing embryo manufactures this part of the placenta (the chorionic villi), these cells have the same genetic makeup as the fetal cells. Hence, any abnormality in the sample cells implies a genetic defect in the fetus.

The advantage of chorionic villus sampling is that it is done between the 9th and 12th week of pregnancy, several weeks earlier than amniocentesis can be performed. The test results come back much faster, 48 to 72 hours compared to one to two weeks for amniocentesis. Parents can learn much sooner whether their baby has a hereditary disease and have the option of an abortion much earlier in the pregnancy. For parents who know that they are carriers of devastating inheritable illnesses such as cystic fibrosis or Huntington's chorea, earlier diagnosis can mean earlier relief from anxiety and worry.

Chorionic villus sampling is not yet widely available because researchers are still evaluating the potential risks, particularly a slightly increased risk of miscarriage compared to amniocentesis.

Alpha-fetoprotein or AFP is a substance made by the fetus as it grows. Some of this protein passes into the amniotic fluid, which bathes the fetus, and a smaller amount crosses the placenta into the mother's blood. If the fetus has a **neural tube defect**, meaning the brain and/or spinal cord are not developing normally, the AFP levels are abnormally high. Abnormally low AFP levels may indicate other prenatal problems.

The **fetal activity test** is a fancy name for a very simple procedure. An expectant mother merely keeps a record of the number of times she feels fetal movement within a certain time period. The amount that a fetus moves is a rough indication of his well-being.

The **nonstress test** monitors changes in the fetus's heart rate with his movements. Ultrasonic monitors placed on the mother's abdomen detect the fetal heart sounds. The mother notes when she feeels the fetus move. Just as your pulse quickens with exercise, the fetus's heart rate should briefly increase with movement.

The **stress test**, or oxytocin challenge test, is similar to the nonstress test—except that the pregnant woman is injected with a small amount of oxytocin. Oxytocin is a naturally occurring hormone that causes the uterus to contract. The fetal heart rate and uterine contractions are monitored and recorded. Normally, the fetal heart rate drops briefly when the uterus contracts, and then quickly recovers. Other patterns may be abnormal and signify that the fetus may not respond well to the stress of labor.

malpractice liability. For example, if ultrasound can indeed be done without significant risk, should it be offered to all patients?

Likewise, parents are faced with issues that didn't exist a generation ago. If a diagnostic procedure is available to them, should they take advantage of it? Birth defects are rare. But if there is any chance of something being wrong with their baby, should the parents try to find out? Normal test results do not guarantee that nothing is wrong with the baby, only that the baby does not have any of the abnormalities current technology can detect.

Probably the most important question is, If something is wrong, do the parents really want to know? Knowing means making difficult decisions like aborting a fetus with a terminal disease versus carrying the pregnancy to term only to lose the baby shortly after birth.

The ethics of obstetrical intervention of any kind are complicated, and one can easily become quagmired. You are entitled to your own opinions. Knowing some of the facts helps you draw more logical conclusions. If you find yourself at cross-purposes with your adult children, try to be tactful. Difficult ethical considerations are fraught with underlying volatile emotions.

Whenever possible, try to be supportive of the parents in the choices they make during the pregnancy. They will appreciate your trust. Your vote of confidence will also pave the way for an amicable atmosphere when you begin your new career as grandparent.

Chapter Three

GETTING READY

Mentally Preparing for Your Rite of Passage into Grandparenthood

As soon as your first grandchild is conceived, so is your career as a grandparent. Remember back to when you first learned that you were soon to be a parent. You probably started to form mental images of yourself in your new role. You envisioned yourself sitting Madonna-like with your newborn nestled in the crook of your arm. Or perhaps you were a realist who foresaw yourself metamorphosed from a nattily dressed career person who dined at fancy restaurants into a bleary-eyed creature in spit-up-splotched clothes struggling with endless mounds of dirty laundry and separating squabbling children.

Just as learning of your incipient grandparenthood triggers memories of your own parenthood, it will also prompt you to mentally rehearse your role as a grandparent. You might find yourself reflecting upon things that your own grandparents did with you when you were a child. You might think about how your parents behaved in the role of grandparents to your children.

As you reminisce about these models of grandparents, ask yourself how you think these folks performed in their roles. What kind of style did they use: strict and authoritarian, aloof and uninvolved, playful and companionate? What things did they do that you didn't like: criticize you, lecture your children, interfere too much, or fail to get involved enough? What kind of grandparent do you hope to be?

Next, ask yourself how you feel about being a grandparent. Most people have conflicting feelings when it comes to the important things in life. Expectant grandparents often feel great joy: happiness for the parents; contentment in knowing your superior genes will be recycled; delight at knowing you will have the chance to recapture cherished sensations, such as melting inside when small arms clasp your neck; mirth upon realizing your adult children are going to gain an appreciation for the spectrum of human emotion they once invoked in you; and satisfaction in knowing you will soon be even more loved and needed.

In the midst of celebrating your new position in the family tree, you may solemnly become mindful of your inescapable physical mortality. You may also feel the nibble of doubts, worries, and insecurities such as, "Do the parents have enough financial security to support a baby? Will my daughter let me see my grandchildren often enough? Just how much babysitting will I be asked to do? Will my cat end up in the drier? Is my crystal in peril? What about my new white carpet?..."

After you acknowledge your more amorphous feelings about becoming a grandparent, you can start to focus on the more concrete decisions. One of the most important questions to answer is, What will my role be around the time of the birth? You will ultimately need to discuss this issue with the parents.

But first of all, ask yourself, "Do I like babies?" If the answer is "No, the sound of crying, the smell of baby excrement, and the sight of curdled regurgitated milk is enough to make me move to Death Valley," then you should not offer to come and help the new family. The arrival of a new baby causes enough normal familial tensions without the presence of a grandparent who really cannot tolerate infants.

If the answer is, "Yes, I am the sort of person who positively melts into a jiggling blob of gelatin whenever I catch sight of an infant," then you have a whole series of other questions to answer. Do you want to be present at or soon after the birth? When would the parents want you to join them?

41

Sometimes parents and grandparents don't know how they are going to feel until the momentous occasion arrives. An expectant couple might tell the grandparents not to come until several days after the birth when the new family is more settled.

Inexplicably, as soon as the baby is delivered, these new parents might desperately want all the grandparents to come and admire their little marvel as soon as possible. When the grandparents are telephoned and they hear their grandbaby's mewing cries in the background, they may likewise develop an urgent impulse to hop on the next plane. The message here is to make tentative plans, but to allow for flexibility when surging hormones cause people to give in to their instincts and emotions. When you and the parents have agreed that your presence is desirable sometime around the birth, consider these details. If you don't live in the same town, where will you stay? If the parents graciously offer to put you up, ask yourself whether you will truly be comfortable staying there. Maybe you have graduated from roughing it in sleeping bags or sleeping on a hideabed in the living room. Perhaps you'd prefer having your own room—a haven for times when you or the parents need to be alone.

A crucial issue is how well you get along with the parents. If you have trouble getting along with your adult children, staying in the same house is bound to create tension. The arrival of a grandchild often strengthens attachments between parents and grandparents. But don't count on this phenomenon to completely patch up preexisting intergenerational static. Start now to make amends. From your point of view, a good relationship with the parents is key if you want to see your grandchildren.

After you have analyzed your relationship with your children and have figured out the logistics of where you will stay and when you will arrive, think about how you would like to help the new family. Next, ask the parents what they would like you to do to help. If you had imagined yourself ensconced in a rocking chair with your grandbaby while the parents had expected that *you* would cook, shop, and tidy the house while they rested and cuddled their newborn—then you are all headed for a storm of postnatal frustrations, disappointments, and resentments. If you have neither the energy nor the desire to shoulder household chores (nor the financial wherewithal to sponsor domestic help), admit it now. It is far better to discuss this in advance.

Having mentally resolved these basic issues that will govern your first days as a grandparent, you can now consider some of the more tangible things you can do during the pregnancy.

Visualization

One technique you can use to mentally prepare yourself for grandparenthood is called visualization. What you need is a comfortable, quiet place where you will not be disturbed by the outside world. Find a comfortable position either sitting or lying down. Close your eyes. Feel that your body is relaxed. Turn your mind into a blank screen. Upon that screen form images of positive situations for the parents, your grandbaby, and yourself as a grandparent.

For example, visualize an uncomplicated birth resulting in a healthy grandchild. See yourself happily playing with your grandbaby, good naturedly helping the parents, laughing with the entire family. Thoughts often find a way of fulfilling themselves. If you wish for positive outcomes, think positive thoughts.

While in this peaceful state, you might ask yourself the questions mentioned earlier. When you have finished visualizing joyful future scenarios, slowly return to your usual pace. For instance, while your eyes are still closed, count backwards from ten. Open your eyes. Slowly move your arms and legs. When you are ready, gently get up and go back to your usual routine.

Helping the Expectant Mother

Some pregnant women find it difficult to justify spending much money on clothes they will wear for a limited period of time, yet feel much better wearing maternity clothes. Although their husbands' baggy shirts and sweaters might fit comfortably, such attire makes for less than stylish evening wear. If you know your pregnant daughter's tastes, you can buy her maternity clothes. Otherwise, take your daughter shopping or give her money earmarked for maternity clothes.

Pregnancy puts increased demands on a woman's body. There are a number of ways you can help. You can lend a hand in household chores or offer to hire domestic help. If your pregnant

daughter already has a child or two, you might offer to baby-sit or pay a baby-sitter.

Pregnant women, especially during the first pregnancy, often worry about things that they consider too trivial to share with their doctor such as, "Will I resemble a deflated balloon after the birth? Will my hemorrhoidal discomfort ever abate? Will I be a good mother? Is the article I saw at the check-out counter about the woman who was pregnant with one baby for four years true? Could this happen to me?" You can offer emotional support by listening to her concerns and offering appropriate reassurances (when you can do so with honesty). Reinforce her feelings of womanliness and glowing vitality.

Toward the end of the pregnancy, many women find that each day seems like a plodding eternity. You can offer healthy distractions such as taking your daughter to lunch, going for walks together, sending her absorbing novels. (Avoid stories in which the heroine suffers through a prolonged and painful birth.) Remember that calling too frequently to find out if your grandchild is born *yet* will only intensify your daughter's impatience and also make her quite irritable with you.

Helping the Expectant Father

During the pregnancy, an expectant father is also preparing for his new role. Today's society is starting to acknowledge men's emotional reactions to this rite of passage. Traditionally, pregnant women have received most of the sympathy. In some ways, men have been fortunate. Strangers usually do not pat expectant fathers on the belly, nor do acquaintances inquire about their gastronomic functions.

Most men have ambivalent feelings about their impending fatherhood: feelings of pride in their virility, excitement at the thought of playing touch football with their offspring, anxiety over future financial burdens, and trepidation at the seemingly unremitting responsibilities involved in rearing a child. You grandfathers probably shared some of these feelings. Just admitting that you also had conflicting reactions to being a father can make your son feel better.

Modern fathers now have the privilege of being more involved in the pregnancy, the birth, and the raising of their children. Research shows that a father's support of his mate during the pregnancy and birth, and his intimate involvement in child rearing, can yield dramatically positive effects on his children.

Some men may feel overwhelmed by expectations to be nurturing and sensitive toward their spouses and children *and* to keep pace with their previous responsibilities at the workplace. Although you expectant grandfathers may not have felt pressured by the same expectations, encouraging your son to air his angst can be very therapeutic. You grandmothers can also encourage your sons to be loving and supportive husbands and fathers.

46

As you well know, each new family member adds an extra financial burden. If it is within your budget, you can help by lending the parents money, paying medical expenses, buying baby paraphernalia, and so on.

Guide to Baby Products

You don't have to be a Rockefeller to provide your grand-child with valued treasures. To minimize expenses, you can buy used baby equipment and furniture, borrow from friends, search your attic and basement for keepsakes, or get out your hammer and knitting needles.

Before you spend too much time thinking about what you'd like to give your grandbaby, talk to the parents about what they need. Then, you can use the following list of baby paraphernalia to help guide you.

☐ **Clothes.** A general rule is not to acquire a lot of infant-sized clothes because your average grandbaby will quickly outgrow them. Also, for most brands of infant clothing, the advertised size fits a child *up to* that age. All a newborn needs in the way of clothes are a few cotton shirts, gowns, or sleepers. Two or three receiving blankets and one or two sweaters are useful for extra warmth. In an improvement over the basic baby bunt-ing, a couple of companies have designed baby bags—tiny sleeping bags divided at the bottom to ac-commodate little legs. If your grandbaby lives in a place where winters are chilly, a baby bag is great for keeping him warm on outings.

☐ **Shoes.** Your grandchild will not need shoes until she is walking. Children actually learn to walk better in bare or stocking feet so they can grip the floor with their tiny toes. They need shoes primarily to protect their feet from sharp objects. Unless your grandchild has an orthopedic problem, she does not need stiff, high-topped leather shoes. Most experts recommend well-fitting, flexible shoes, for example, your basic sneaker.

☐ **Furniture.** In our culture, most babies sleep in bassinets, cradles, or cribs (although tiny infants won't complain about sleeping in a clean, padded drawer or box). Bas-sinets and cradles are quickly outgrown, but are useful if the parents want to keep the baby near them. Portable cribs are handy for traveling (especially for trips to your house).

If you are considering handing down a used crib, first check to see that it complies with current safety codes. Crib slats should be tightly in place and no more than 2⅜ inches apart (so your grandbaby can't get her head trapped between them). The crib side should move up and down easily and lock in place firmly when in the up mode. Check that the crib has no sharp edges. The crib mattress (standard size of 27¼ by 51⅝ inches) should fit so snugly that your grandbaby couldn't possible get her head caught between the crib side and the mattress.

A portable playpen can substitute for a crib, particularly when the family goes visiting. As with cribs, playpens should have securely locking sides and no potential spaces where your grandbaby can entrap his head or limbs. Many child-care experts feel that prolonged confinement in a playpen impedes an infant's exploration and thus, his development. And because playpens take up a significant amount of space, some parents prefer to simply let their baby play on a blanket on the floor of a child-proofed room (see Chapter thirteen for more on child-proofing).

Other useful nursery furnishings include a chest of drawers, a small bookshelf, a lamp, a toy-chest, and a rocking chair. Some parents like to have a changing table (where the baby lies during diaper changes). Bathinets have gone the way of the victrola, having been replaced by inflatable baby baths, small plastic tubs, and large sponges molded to fit an infant that can be set on the counter, or in the tub or sink.

Infant-sized furniture is another category that encompasses a variety of places to safely (in the presence of a vigilant adult) seat your grandbaby: infant seats, bouncy chairs, high-chairs, and little seats that hook onto a sturdy table. The latter two types of chairs require an infant who has enough torso strength to sit up (which usually doesn't happen until six months of age). All of these miniature seats should have a lap belt to prevent your grandbaby from sliding out.

☐ **Bedding.** Your grandbaby will need bedding, including a couple of crib sheets, two waterproof pads, two mattress pads, bumper pads, and a couple of washable quilts or blankets.

☐ **Outings.** In the United States, prams and baby carriages are sighted with the same frequency as the Model T Ford. These bulky dinosaurs have largely been supplanted by more lightweight, streamlined strollers. Strollers range widely in quality and price from Mercedes equivalents to V.W.-type umbrella strollers. A good, sturdy, middle-of-the-road stroller should have an adjustable back rest, a canopy, and good-sized wheels that maneuver curbs and bumps and turn easily. Also, the stroller should fold up small enough to be stowed in the car or on an airplane.

Alternative modes of transporting a baby include the front carrier and the backpack. The front carrier is useful for infants too young to sit up. The baby is held in place close to the adult's chest by a cloth harness. Although most small babies seem to find this womb-like environment comforting, some infants struggle against the confinement. Backpacks are more comfortable from the sherpa's point of view, but require that the baby sit up fairly well.

If your grandbaby goes anywhere in an automobile, he should be safely strapped into his car seat. All states have mandatory car-seat laws. If you pick up a used car seat, make sure that it meets current federal safety standards.

You might feel that your grandbaby would be much more comfortable traveling in a car in the arms of a caring adult. However, to do so would be putting your grandbaby at an unnecessary risk of injury or death in the event of an accident (and motor vehicle accidents represent the major cause of death of young children). Holding your grandbaby in your arms greatly increases the force with which he might strike the dash or windshield should the car stop suddenly.

☐ **Toys, books, records, and tapes.** Many parenting and grandparenting books have long lists of recommended toys, books, and records/tapes for children according to their developmental abilities. When buying toys for your grandbaby, think of things that will stimulate his sensory faculties (toy animals or quilts made of varying textured materials to touch; unbreakable mirrors and high contrast mobiles hung just out of reach but within view to look at; music boxes or soothing music on record or tape for listening pleasure) and physical development (smooth, nontoxic objects small enough to grasp, suck, and shake, but large enough that they can't be swallowed or choked upon). See Chapter nine for more information about infant development.

☐ **Miscellaneous gifts.** Portable humidifiers can be beneficial (if kept scrupulously clean), particularly in dry climates, if your grandbaby has a respiratory illness. If the parents elect to use cloth diapers, you could offer to pay for a diaper service. (See Chapter ten for more on cloth versus disposable diapers.) Parenting books and a baby book or calendar for recording development milestones can help the parents stay mentally organized during those first years.

A very special gift is a grandparents' memory book. You can even buy books that outline for you all of the things your grandchildren would want to know about you. All you have to do is supply the appropriate information and photographs. Although time consuming, a memory book is a wonderful way of preserving family history.

If you or the parents don't own a camera, you will all wish you did when grandbaby arrives. Be sure to have plenty of film on hand. Blank photo albums make practical gifts for both you and the parents. (And if the new baby is not the first born, he'll later appreciate incentives to be photographed as much as Big Sister or Brother.)

If you *really* want to spend some money, you can consider buying a camcorder. If you don't want to make the investment, you can always rent a video camera to document your grandchildren's development and to dynamically capture special occasions on tape.

Summary of Baby Equipment

Clothes
4 shirts
4 gowns or sleepers
2 coveralls
3 receiving blankets
2 sweaters

Furniture
crib
bassinet or cradle
dresser
changing table
lamp
rocking chair
bookshelf
toy chest
playpen
infant seat
high-chair or seat that hooks onto table
baby bath

Outings
stroller
backpack
front carrier
car seat
baby bag or bunting

Toys
unbreakable mirror
mobiles
rattles
music boxes
tapes and records
books with cardboard pages
toys with interesting textures

Bedding
2 crib sheets
2 mattress pads
2 waterproof pads
2 quilts or blankets

Miscellaneous
humidifier
diaper service
baby book
parenting books
grandparents' memory book
camera
film

Chapter Four

CHANGING FASHIONS IN CHILDBIRTH

A Brief History of Obstetrics

If you could have breezed into the local bookstore two hundred years ago, you would not have had much luck finding a book covering changes in the care of women during pregnancy and childbirth. That's because nothing had changed in this arena of health care for thousands of years. It was not until this century that obstetrics underwent a metamorphosis and emerged a gainful business.

Back in the good ol' days, women found themselves to be "with child" frequently, because birth control was even more primitive than it is now. A woman became pregnant in the usual fashion. What little information or misinformation she gathered about pregnancy and childbirth was often gleaned from old wives' tales. No health care professionals in crisp white coats monitored her blooming progress. When she went into labor, she was attended by another woman, hopefully an experienced midwife. The midwife might even have been her own mother! (You expectant grandmothers may be relieved to know that you needn't rush out and take a crash course in midwifery. Read on.)

From the earliest recorded time until the 1800s, midwives were, without exception, females. Physicians, an exclusively male group until recent times, considered routine childbirth outside their realm. Furthermore, society considered the practice of obstetrics by men a moral impropriety. Women were extremely modest; their husbands violently objected to the mere thought of another man having anything to do with their wives' sacred parts. Indeed, feelings of decorum ran so strongly that, in 1552, a male physician was burned at the stake for posing as a woman in order to attend a birth.

No doubt discouraged at this juncture in history from turning obstetrics into a lucrative practice, physicians attended births only when called to treat complications. Midwives continued to deliver the majority of American babies well into the 1900s. They not only attended women during labor and delivery, but also made themselves popular by participating in household chores such as cleaning, cooking, and settling the newborn baby.

For several reasons, the number of midwives in the United States progressively dwindled:

• Unlike many European countries, the United States lacked central governmental support for the education, training, and licensure of midwives.

• Beginning in the late 1800s, physicians, who were becoming more involved in the practice of obstetrics, publicly questioned the expertise of midwives.

• As politicians joined the campaign against midwives, many states banned midwifery and legally prosecuted practicing midwives.

• After World War I immigration declined, thus cutting off an important source of new midwives.

• Although births still occurred primarily in the home, it became a status symbol to procure the assistance of a physician rather than a midwife.

Given the unfavorable climate, the number of midwives practicing in the United States declined from 20,700 in 1948 to 2,880 in 1972. Eventually, physician attendance became standard during childbirth (until the natural childbirth movement revived the practice of midwifery).

With the replacement of midwives by physicians came many changes in the manner in which children were brought into this world. First, physicians seeking relief from their own back pain insisted that women labor and deliver in the *lithotomy position*. Lying on her back with her feet in stirrups not only was uncomfortable for the woman but also compromised the blood flow to her baby and opposed the laws of gravity and nature. From the doctor's point of view, this position permitted easier access to the birth canal and advanced the implementation of various obstetrical procedures.

One of these procedures was *forceps extraction* of the baby. Forceps have long metal blades to grasp the baby's head as it enters the birth canal and thus expedite her descent. For a time, newborns often sported transient black and blue "birthmarks" on either side of their heads. In the 1920s, *episiotomy*, an incision to enlarge the opening of the birth canal, became popular as a way to facilitate the use of forceps. Although sometimes genuinely necessary, neither of these procedures added to a woman's perception of pleasure during the birth.

Luckily for all expectant women of the time, the introduction of pain medicines roughly coincided with the advent of invasive obstetrics. Because pain medicines were administered in the hospital, middle- and upper- class women of the 1920s flocked to these institutions to deliver their babies.

Before this time, only poor women and unwed mothers sought hospital deliveries. Initially, hospital births were riskier than home births for both mother and child because of the higher rate of infectious diseases. Later, physicians adopted the highly technical protocol of washing their hands between patients. The advent of antibiotics and blood banking during the 1940s further increased the safety of hospital birth.

After physicians replaced midwives and hospitals replaced the home as a place to deliver, birth became a process referred to by empathetic health professionals as "knock 'em out, drag 'em out" or "cut, pull, sew." The following describes standard obstetrical procedure during the middle of this century:

• A woman was admitted to the hospital at the first sign of labor and was so heavily sedated that she was unable to appreciate contractions, pain, or anything else.

• She was left to labor alone on the maternity ward, save for a dozen or so other stuporous, laboring women.

• For the actual birth of her baby, she was moved to a cold, sterile delivery room and "put to sleep."

• Just in case she regained consciousness, she was often handcuffed to the surgical table to prevent her from moving during the delivery.

• Because a semi-conscious woman can't very well push out her baby, the doctor performed an episiotomy and extracted the baby with forceps.

• The pain medications often inhibited the woman's normal uterine contractions, not only slowing down labor but also impeding the delivery of the placenta and increasing the risk of hemorrhage. To remedy this situation, the placenta was often extracted by hand (ouch!) and medications (ergot—and later Pitocin) were given to stimulate uterine contractions. Intervention begat intervention.

• Because the baby had been dosed with the same medications as the mother, he emerged blue and limp, too groggy to

57

take that first breath. Hence came the tradition of the physician dangling the newborn by the heels and whacking his backside to stimulate breathing and other signs of life.

• Burly nurses wearing funny hats then whisked the babe away to a nursery.

• Because fathers were obliged to smoke cigars in the waiting room and mothers were communing with the stars, neither had the opportunity to participate in the birth process or in the early care of their newborn.

In the 1940s an English physician, Grantly Dick-Read, noted that not all women experienced childbirth as a painful process. Treatises on the history of obstetrics do not discuss whether these women might have been missing entire portions of their nervous systems. At any rate, he theorized that fear led to tension and that tension, in turn, led to increased pain. He developed a method of childbirth that aimed at interrupting the fear-tension-pain cycle. He taught his patients relaxation and breathing exercises. Furthermore, rather than medicating his patients and leaving them alone, he actually attended his patients throughout their labor—encouraging them all the while.

In 1947, Yale University Medical School received a grant to study the Read method. In addition to practicing Dr. Dick-Read's techniques, the researchers introduced the notion of allowing babies to "room-in" with their mothers instead of being sent to the nursery. Also, mothers were sheltered from the legions of infant formula sales representatives lurking about hospitals and instead were encouraged to breast-feed rather than bottle-feed their infants. Both parents and physicians involved in this study praised the Read method.

In another radical departure from obstetrical routine, a Colorado physician, Robert Bradley, made another contribution to the prepared or "natural" childbirth movement by allowing fathers to be in the delivery room. His dumbfounded colleagues threatened that fathers would faint when they saw that the baby comes into this world along with other assorted fluids, would bring germs into the delivery room, and would file lawsuits.

Amazingly enough, fathers failed to live up to these expectations. Most of them not only maintained consciousness throughout the birth, but actually enjoyed the experience. (It is a scientifically proven fact that labor and delivery generally produce less discomfort for the father than for the mother.) Furthermore, mothers found the support their mates offered enormously helpful. Dr. Bradley delivered some 9,000 babies without the use of pain medicines—by either patient or doctor. (The mothers did have the option of receiving pain medications.)

Since that time, other natural childbirth methods have been developed. Some names you might hear include the Lamaze, Kitzinger, and Leboyer methods. Prepared childbirth really caught on during the 1970s as both the lay public and the medical profession began to suspect that other methods besides drugs were effective in providing pain relief for childbirth. (Not to mention the widely accepted historical fact that, during the seventies, young adults felt compelled to do most things as differently as possible than their parents had done.)

Presently, most hospitals and birthing centers offer classes in prepared childbirth for expectant parents. (And some even offer special classes for grandparents.) Prepared childbirth means that parents are informed about the process of pregnancy and labor, and are taught delivery and comfort measures to help them cope. Most childbirth classes borrow from several methods, but all include education, controlled breathing, and other relaxation exercises. The central idea is that a woman who understands what is happening to her body and is able to relax will experience less pain during her labor.

A "coach"—expectant father, friend, or relative —attends the classes with the mother. This support person is trained to be sensitive to the woman's needs during labor and delivery, and to respond by initiating the appropriate relaxation and comfort techniques. More specifically, the coach is supposed to respond to the mother's moans and groans by doing touchy-feely things like massaging tense body parts, playing soft music, and repeating in a hypnotic voice that although her contractions are so strong the entire bed is shaking, she should try not to regard them as painful. No longer are fathers encouraged to read *Trout* magazine, eat popcorn, and watch baseball on television during the birth of their children.

As though the father didn't have enough to do coaching the mother through childbirth, he is also expected to participate with the mother in early parent-infant bonding. That means that, starting from moment one, the parents should coo like doves, ogle, and fondle their newborn. Otherwise, the child might grow up to be a maladjusted, psychically wounded person. (For more on bonding, see Chapter six.)

After pointing out the complications inherent in a drug and intervention-oriented childbirth, it is important to mention that advances in obstetric procedures have spared the lives of many women and babies. At times, medical intervention is not only indicated, but it is lifesaving.

Also, modern pain medications have fewer deleterious side effects (for both mother and baby) and play an important role in making difficult births more tolerable. Prepared childbirth instructors should explain the range of interventions and medications to parents so they can make informed decisions. A woman who judges that she needs pain relief is not first required to sign a form promising to feel forever guilty.

Try not to feel offended or disappointed if your children want to have their babies in a radically different fashion. Some parents have wholeheartedly embraced the prepared childbirth movement with its emphasis on avoidance of unnecessary medical procedures. They have turned to midwife delivery, home births, or birthing centers as alternatives to standard hospital births. They have chosen to breast-feed rather than bottle-feed their infants.

On the other hand, your children may feel more secure in a traditional hospital setting, surrounded by high-tech monitors and modern pharmaceuticals. The key is that parents now have more options when it comes to birth. Contemporary parents have the luxury of tailoring their birth experience using any combination of natural childbirth techniques and obstetrical technology.

If you want to know more about "modern" childbirth, ask your expectant children. They will no doubt be pleased that you are interested and can direct you to their favorite books or even invite you to attend a prenatal class with them.

Chapter Five

THE BIRTH DAY

Who Delivers Your Grandbaby?

People with a wide variety of professional backgrounds, including firemen, taxi drivers, flight attendants, and grandparents, have delivered babies. Today's average expectant mother hopes that the medical expert who cared for her throughout the pregnancy will also deliver her baby.

If you had your babies during the forties and fifties, the skilled professional probably came in the form of a male physician. Because the natural childbirth movement helped repopularize midwifery, expectant parents now can choose between a physician or a midwife.

The doctor may just as likely be a woman as a man. Usually the physician is a family doctor with lots of experience delivering babies, or is an obstetrician.

The midwife may be a nurse midwife or a lay midwife. Nurse midwives are registered nurses who have completed a certified nurse midwifery program. Lay midwives learn their midwifery skills largely by apprenticeship. Regulations and licensure of midwives vary from state to state.

Every doctor or midwife has his or her philosophy about obstetrics. Some practitioners tend to be more "interventionist," meaning they are more likely to make use of advanced technical procedures.

Other practitioners prefer to "let nature take her course," interfering only when deemed absolutely necessary to protect the mother and/or baby. Midwives generally fall into this latter category. They are also more likely to assist the mother during the labor as well as the delivery of the baby.

A woman who is considered to be at high risk for a problematic pregnancy and birth, and hence more likely to need medical intervention, is usually encouraged to seek care from an obstetrician, rather than from a family doctor or midwife. Fortunately, most healthy women can deliver normal babies with little or no obstetrical intervention.

Where Does the Birth Take Place?

Due to unforeseen circumstances, a woman occasionally does not give birth in the anticipated setting. Fortunately, babies are hardy, instinctual creatures who are almost as well versed in the art of birth as an obstetrician or midwife. Even in the back seat of an automobile, the average baby can practically deliver herself.

Although most deliveries still take place in the hospital, expectant parents now have other options and can chose the one that best fits their ideals. The usual birth settings include the traditional hospital delivery room, the home, "alternative" birth centers within a hospital, and "free-standing" birth centers separate from a hospital.

Traditional Hospital Delivery

Because it is likely that you grandparents delivered your babies in hospitals, you remember the birth well and no further discussion is necessary, right? If the answer is no, you are in good company. As fathers, you were probably excluded from the delivery room and, as mothers, you were probably heavily sedated.

Now, parents giving birth in hospitals are more likely to recount their adventures to their children. ("You were real cute, kinda scrunched-looking and covered with blood, and the placenta was just beautiful...") Fathers are often actively involved in assisting mothers during labor and delivery and mothers are usually awake and alert for the birth.

67

The standard procedure during a routine hospital birth is as follows: sometime after a woman goes into labor, she is admitted to a hospital room; rather than taking labor lying down, today's imminently expectant mother can often be seen wobbling around the halls, pausing only to lean against her coach during a contraction. The idea here is that activity hastens labor.

During labor, the muscular contractions of a woman's uterus push her baby downward and dilate the cervix (the outlet from the uterus into the vagina). As labor progresses and the contractions begin to register on the Richter scale, the mother may wish she had enlisted a surrogate mother to have her baby.

Ideally, the father or other "support person" is present to help make her as comfortable as possible. At regular intervals, an obstetrical nurse, doctor, or midwife checks the woman's progress and the baby's well-being as reflected by the heart rate.

By the end of labor, the woman's cervix has dilated to a diameter of ten centimeters (hopefully), allowing her baby to squeeze past into the birth canal. Although she is not in the mood to go anywhere, the mother is hastily transferred to the delivery room—a modified surgical suite full of cold metal, surgical instruments, and bright lights. It is here that she will help push her baby into the waiting hands of the doctor or midwife.

Because the ambiance in the delivery room isn't exactly warm and homey, increasingly hospitals are allowing women to labor, deliver, and recover in the same room. (For more information, see the section on alternative birth centers on page 70.)

Many parents choose hospital delivery because they feel more secure knowing that all the instruments of medical technology, and the expertise to use them, are immediately available should a complication arise. On the other hand, medical procedures are sometimes overutilized in a hospital setting. Some parents feel less in control, and even intimidated or frightened, by medical interventions. Sometimes these interventions are critical to the health of the mother or her baby. Other times, they do more harm than good.

Home Birth

During the mid 1970s, the home again became an acceptable place to have a baby. As the natural childbirth movement caught on, more parents desired to give birth in a familiar, comfortable, private setting, free from unnecessary medical intervention. This place was home sweet home.

To be a good candidate for home birth, a woman must be in good health, have no history of complications of pregnancy or childbirth, have good family support, and live close to a hospital. Parents are advised to attend childbirth education classes and follow routine prenatal care with the physician or midwife who will attend the birth.

You may well wonder, "Are home births really safe?" Although the issue of safety is controversial, several studies have shown home births to be as safe as hospital deliveries. The slight risk of a complication requiring transfer to a hospital is balanced by the risk of a problem being caused by unnecessary medical intervention during a hospital birth. Parents must then weigh their apprehensions about delivering at home without rapid ac-

69

cess to emergency medical procedures against their concerns about being subjected to hospital regulations and interventions.

Alternative Birth Centers

During the late 1970s, alternative birth centers were created to combine the attractive features of home births and hospital deliveries—to combine a warm, comfortable, informal environment with the availability of technical medical services.

Birth centers may be either separate from or located within the hospital. The rooms are decorated to resemble bedrooms and may include accoutrements such as plants, stereo equipment, and comfortable chairs or hideabeds for weary fathers. (Actually, these rooms resemble only the bedrooms of people who are fastidiously clean, favor Spartan decoration, and keep medical equipment tucked away in drawers.)

Often, the mother's bed looks like an ordinary twin bed that, a la James Bond technology, converts into a "birthing chair" for the delivery. This enables the woman to assume positions that facilitate birth much better than the supine position does.

Women are allowed to labor, deliver, and recover in the same room. Hospital rules and routine interventions are kept to a minimum. The physicians, midwives, and nurses who staff these birth centers are supportive of natural childbirth, early bonding between parents and newborn, and breast-feeding.

Whether the parents enlist the help of a physician or midwife, whether they elect to give birth at the Mayo Clinic or in a teepee, you will (hopefully) find a way to be supportive even if you wouldn't do things that way for a million dollars.

Medical Interventions

In the event that you are present during a hospital birth, you may want to prepare yourself by knowing a little about the more common medical interventions. The frequency of their use depends both upon how reliant the physician is upon medical technology and how problematic the birth is.

☐ *An Intravenous (I.V.) line* consists of a narrow plastic or metal catheter (tube) inserted into a vein (usually in the

70

back of the hand or wrist) and connected by tubing to a fluid-filled bag or bottle hanging on a stand. Some practitioners start I.V.s routinely on all laboring women in the event that an emergency arises calling for rapid administration of drugs or fluids. Others only place I.V.s as needed.

☐ *Fetal monitors* utilize electronic devices to graphically depict the mother's uterine contractions and the baby's heart rate. The baby's heart rate provides a rough indication of how well he is coping with the stresses of labor. If the results of fetal monitoring are questionable, a drop of blood can be taken from the baby's scalp to make sure she is getting enough oxygen.

☐ *Forceps* are long metal instruments reminiscent of salad spoons that can be used to pull the baby's head down the birth canal during a difficult delivery.

A more modern adaptation of forceps delivery is "vacuum extraction." A silastic cap is placed over the baby's head and suction is applied to literally vacuum the baby out of the birth canal.

☐ *Episiotomy* is a small incision made from the bottom of the opening of the vagina (birth canal) toward the anus. (This is the procedure that makes some fathers wish they had been relegated to the waiting room.) Theoretically, episiotomy is performed only when the emerging baby is stretching the tissues so much that they would otherwise tear, or if forceps must be introduced into the vagina to deliver the baby. Although the frequency of routine episiotomies has decreased with the advent of prepared childbirth, nearly 90 percent of all first-time mothers delivering in hospital will undergo this surgery.

☐ *Pitocin.* This drug can be given intravenously to stimulate uterine contractions. Pitocin is often used to initiate labor, to augment uterine contractions that have waned, or to treat postpartum (after the birth) hemorrhage. A common side effect of pitocin is that a woman's contractions are more uncomfortable—making her feel less in control of her labor, more like a denizen of Mount Saint Helens during the eruption.

☐ *Cesarean section.* Cesarean birth means that the baby is delivered via a surgical incision in the mother's abdomen because a complication makes vaginal delivery risky or impossible. Due to various social and medical factors, the rate of Cesarean section has increased from 3 to 5 percent in the 1950s to 24 percent of all U.S. births as of 1988. This rate surpasses that of any other country.

Relatively recently, obstetricians have been making the surgical incision horizontally (rather than vertically) through the lower abdomen and uterus. Not only is this "bikini" incision cosmetically preferable, but it is less likely to weaken the uterus. This gives the woman a chance to deliver vaginally during subsequent births.

Many women undergo Cesarean section with epidural or spinal anesthesia (see next section) so that they are alert for the birth. Fathers are usually allowed to remain with their mates for Cesarean births. (In general, mothers seem to tolerate the surgery better than the fathers).

If your daughter has a Cesarean birth, she may need your support even more than if she had had a normal vaginal delivery. Because her recuperation has been complicated by major surgery, she will need extra help those first weeks at home. Furthermore, she may also have intense feelings of disappointment because the birth did not go as planned. She might even feel she has somehow failed. You can be a great source of comfort just by letting her talk about her feelings.

☐ *Pain medications.* The goal of pain relief has changed in the past few decades. Most modern mothers are alert for their babies' first meal, rather than for their babies' first steps. Because of an awareness of their potential side effects on the mother and baby, drugs that cause deep sedation or general anesthesia are now rarely used. Pain relief can be tailored to meet the needs of the individual patient. Several types of pain relief during birth are currently available.

1) *Analgesics* work by increasing the woman's tolerance or threshold for pain. Narcotics (substances with a morphine-like action) are usually employed for analgesia during labor. Short-acting narcotics have been developed that decrease the risk that the baby will be groggy at the time of delivery. Sedatives such as barbiturates are now rarely used. Mild tranquilizers may be given if a woman is unusually anxious.

2) *Anesthesia* means "loss of feeling." Anesthetic agents can act to cause loss of sensation locally or generally. During *general anesthesia*, the patient is "put to sleep," typically by inhaling a gas. This method is usually reserved for Cesarean sections, particularly if they are emergency procedures.

With *regional anesthesia* the medicine acts to cause loss of sensation in a limited area. One type of regional anesthesia is *spinal anesthesia*. A needle is inserted between the vertebrae in the low back into the fluid-filled space surrounding the spinal cord and an anesthetic medicine is injected. The mother becomes numb and unable to move from the waist downward (which can be problematic if the woman wants to actively participate in the delivery).

In *epidural anesthesia,* the anesthetic agent is injected into the space outside the spinal cord. Epidurals are frequently used for Cesarean births and for pain relief during labor. One advantage over spinal anesthesia is that epidural anesthesia usually does not cause transient paralysis of the lower extremities, allowing the woman to help push her baby down the birth canal.

Local anesthetics can be injected directly into the nerves around the cervix to block pain during labor or into the tissues at the bottom of the vagina if an episiotomy must be performed.

Diminished pain perception can sometimes be achieved through hypnosis or accupuncture during labor and delivery.

The Grandparents' Role During the Birth of a Grandchild

In this chapter little mention was made of grandparents. Unless you have been asked to attend the birth, your role will be limited. (The real challenges for you lie ahead.) Often, parents view birth as an intensely private experience and do not wish to have any spectators (in addition to the nurse, midwife, doctor, anesthesiologist, phlebotomist, and housekeeping personnel...) until after the birth. You should be psychologically prepared for the trend toward expanded paternal involvement in the birth process, so that you do not feel excluded. Of course, you may feel greatly relieved if you are not asked to attend.

If you are in town, other opportunities exist should you feel the need to be of use. Ask the parents whether you might do anything to prepare the household for the new baby, for example, take care of pets, start fixing some meals, or look after any other grandchildren.

Chapter Six

AFTER THE STORK

Early Parent-Infant Bonding

Birth heralds the end of nine months of anticipation and the start of a relationship with a new family member. No wonder the time immediately after birth is so emotionally charged. That birth marks the highlight of a lifetime has never been a secret to parents who were able to be with their newborns. Yet until recently, most doctors and scientists ignored the importance of early parent-infant interactions.

Finally, in 1972, two doctors performed a landmark study comparing differences in the quality of attachment between two groups of mothers and infants. One group of mothers followed normal hospital routine. The mothers saw their babies briefly after birth and every three to four hours thereafter, just long enough for feedings. The other group of mothers was allowed one hour of intimate contact with their newborns soon after birth, plus five hours of extra contact each day until hospital discharge. Observations of this second group of women over the next two years revealed that they cuddled, looked at, and generally interacted more positively with their babies.

Subsequent studies examining the effects of separating mothers and infants at birth have reaffirmed the hypothesis that early and prolonged contact between parents and their newborn leads to increased affection and fewer future behavioral problems. Some experts believe that a critical time for this parent-infant "bonding" coincides with the time soon after birth. Given an opportunity for early contact, a love that unites parents and child takes vigorous hold. It is this ferocious attachment that prevents weary parents from leaving their baby on your doorstep when he cries nonstop, spits up on the Oriental rug, and demolishes family heirlooms.

Natural childbirth facilitates a positive early bonding experience in at least three ways:

1) A calm, unafraid woman who is not groggy with pain medications is more eager to cuddle her newborn.

2) An infant who has not been rendered stuporous by the drugs given her mother during labor is usually in a very quiet, alert state the first hour after birth.

3) A father and/or grandparent who happens to be in the room assisting the mother with the birth (as opposed to pacing the waiting room) has a good chance to hold the newborn. Hence, the important players are all present and receptive to each other.

Given the chance, most parents will instinctively spend the moments immediately after the birth gently touching, crooning to, and maintaining eye-to-eye contact with their newborn. Perhaps even more remarkable is the fact that they are amazingly oblivious to the various bodily substances coating their baby.

Physicians and midwives who are sensitive to the importance of early bonding will place the baby on her mother's bare abdomen or chest immediately after the delivery. This skin-to-skin contact is comforting to both mother and baby (and helps to keep the baby warm).

Also, obstetrical staff often encourage mothers who intend to breast-feed to nurse their infants soon after the birth. Early nursing stimulates the release of the hormone oxytocin from the mother's brain. Oxytocin augments uterine contractions, which decreases the risk of hemorrhage after the birth. Furthermore, the intimacy of nursing is glue in the mother-infant bond.

Baby Rooming-In

Because of the importance of early bonding, many hospitals and birthing centers now allow prolonged intimate contact between parents and infant after birth and encourage rooming-in of mother and infant. Rather than keeping the baby in the nursery, a new mother can elect to have her baby's bassinet placed next to her bed.

Rooming-in does not mean that the mother can never send her baby to the nursery. The system is much more flexible. Whenever a new mother feels she needs a break, she merely requests that the nurses attend her baby in the nursery. In most hospitals and birthing centers, a new mother has the good fortune of being able to spend as much time as she likes with her newborn, provided the baby is healthy.

If a mother chooses to have her baby room-in with her, she has not cut herself off from the benefits of being surrounded by highly trained staff. A pediatrician or family doctor will still examine the baby. Nurses visit the mother and baby at regular intervals 24 hours a day to wake them up and check on various bodily functions.

Aside from facilitating parent-newborn bonding, a major advantage of the baby rooming-in is that fledgling parents have the opportunity to try out their parenting skills *before* they are turned loose on their baby. All kinds of professional advise is on hand should they have problems performing rudimentary tasks such as feeding, diapering, and bathing their newborn. Parents who have had their baby with them since birth are more self-confident when going home than had their newborn been cloistered in the nursery.

Father Rooming-In

Don't be too surprised when you visit your newly born grandbaby and find that not only is the baby rooming-in with the mother, but so is the father! Many hospitals and birthing centers provide a hideabed or the like in the mother's room for weary fathers. These days, it is not uncommon for a first-time

father to remain ensconced until the mother and baby are ready to go home.

You grandparents may find such behavior peculiar. Not long ago, fathers were banned from the recovery room as well as the delivery room. These fathers often first viewed their newborns with faces pressed against nursery windows. Now, they're involved in *everything*.

Grandmothers may feel especially vexed when such attentive fathering continues when the family returns home. How can a grandmother do her traditional duties of helping the mother and cuddling her grandbaby with this interfering man underfoot?

Have patience and don't give up hope. If the father is gainfully employed outside the home, he will eventually be forced to return to work. Although many men are ecstatic participating in the joys of childrearing, most soon recognize its less glamorous aspects and are relieved to escape to their vocations.

Other Policies That Have Changed

Breast-Feeding vs. Bottle-Feeding

The revival of breast-feeding as the preferred method of nourishing a newborn is so important that the better part of Chapter eleven is devoted to this subject.

Circumcision

If you gave birth to any boy babies, they were probably circumcised (i.e., had their foreskins' surgically removed) before leaving the hospital. You might not have even been informed about the procedure. During the fifties, male circumcision was almost universal in English-speaking countries.

In 1971, the American Academy of Pediatrics declared that "there are no valid medical indications for circumcision in the newborn period." Since that time, the circumcision rate in English-speaking countries other than the United States has decreased dramatically. The decline in the United States has been much less remarkable. Here, the majority of baby boys are still routinely circumcised.

This trend will probably continue, because in March 1989 the American Academy of Pediatrics shifted its stance, concluding that "newborn circumcision has potential medical benefits and advantages, as well as inherent disadvantages and risks." The putative advantages are controversial and include a decrease in urinary tract infections in infants, cancer of the penis in adult men, cervical cancer in women with circumcised partners, and a variety of sexually transmitted diseases. The risks of doing the surgery include excessive bleeding, infection, scarring, and pain. In effect, the Academy's position is scientifically neutral — leaving parents in the position of making the decision themselves.

Many parents agonize over the circumcision decision. You can help by being supportive of whatever choice the parents make. Your backing is especially helpful if the verdict means that your grandson's penis will be different from other prominent male relatives. You can tell the parents that your grandson will differ in many other ways from Daddy, Granddaddy, Big Brother.... Your grandson is who is he is regardless of whether or not he has a foreskin.

Length of Hospital/Birthing Center Stay

The length of hospital stay has followed the same trend as swimsuits since the 1950s: both are shrinking. Gone are the days when you stayed in the hospital so long that your baby could practically walk to your room from the nursery to demand a feeding.

If the birth is normal, a first-time mother is usually encouraged to stay in the hospital for 48 to 72 hours. This is enough time for the practitioner to determine whether the mother or baby are likely to have any immediate post-delivery problems and for the staff to teach the parents basic parenting skills and to counsel the mother about diet and exercise.

Most obstetricians tailor the hospital stay to the particular family situation. An experienced mother with good family support may be discharged very early—within 12 to 24 hours after the birth. On the other hand, hospital discharge might be delayed if the mother is exhausted and nervous, the baby is slow to suckle or ill, and so on. A woman who delivers via Cesarean section typically remains in the hospital four to five days.

Earlier hospital discharge has some advantages, such as return to a familiar environment, good food, and other members of the family. It also means less expense. Disadvantages inherent in the homecoming include the domestic duties that have accrued, the adoring but demanding family members who await, and the hordes of friends and relatives who are eager to see the baby.

Visitors

Many hospitals have relaxed their policies about visitors. Visiting hours tend to be longer. Friends as well as immediate family are often allowed to visit. Many hospitals no longer insist that visitors don sterile gowns, but do request that they wash their hands before handling the baby and stay away entirely if they are sick. These more relaxed standards allow you more contact with your grandbaby during those miraculous first days.

During the first weeks after the birth, the baby and his parents need lots of quiet time to recuperate. You can be a big help if you encourage your friends and relatives to refrain from showering the new family with good intentions for a couple of weeks. Tell them the baby will still be quite small, but will have improved in both appearance and behavior by then. In so doing, you will help spare the parents and the baby from needless exhaustion.

Meeting the Needs of Your New Extended Family

The Parents

You can probably still recall something of how you felt your first days at home with your newborn. If you were like most new parents, you felt proud but exhausted (especially the female parent). So, the primary needs of new parents are to savor the triumph of creation by having lots of time to ogle their newborn, and to rest whenever possible. Parents, especially mothers, need to adapt themselves to the baby's sleep-wake cycles (meaning that they should sleep *whenever* the baby sleeps—day or night).

As a grandparent, you can help actualize the parents' needs for rest and time alone with the new baby by

1) giving primary consideration to the parents, rather than the baby (they need your help more than your grandbaby does at this point),

2) shielding the family from visitors (as mentioned above),

3) entertaining other siblings (thereby making other brothers and sisters feel special and relieving the parents' guilt),

4) making yourself scarce at times so the parents can be alone with their baby, and

5) keeping the household running (with or without hired help) so the parents don't have to deal with shopping, cleaning, and cooking (unless they want to).

Another way you can smooth the transition to new parenthood is to watch out for signs of *post-baby blues*. In the wake of a dramatic hormonal upheaval combined with physical and emotional exhaustion, mothers are particularly prone to postpartum depression.

Don't forget that new fatherhood is also an exhilarating and exhausting ordeal, leaving many men with ambivalent feelings. All too often, new fathers are excluded from the attention encircling the mother and the baby.

Coming home from the hospital after being much fussed over by hospital staff and adoring relatives can be an anticlimax for new parents. The euphoria of the first few days often gives way to fatigue, loneliness, and a sense of unremitting responsibility.

Parents may despair if the baby isn't the wished-for gender or is handicapped or ill. Even if the baby is perfect, the parents may worry about such things as being "good" parents, about being tied down, or about how their own relationship will be affected.

So, be on the alert for evidence of "the blues." If your daughter weeps frequently and for no apparent reason (packs her suitcase, books herself on a one-way flight to Australia...), you can be sure she has the blues. Other, more subtle signs in both parents are complaints of insomnia, anxiety, confusion, lack of confidence, and a negative attitude about being a parent. If you aren't sure whether they are suffering from the blues, ask.

You may have to be a little thick-skinned if your children's moodiness interferes with their ability to be gracious and congenial. Grit your teeth and think of such behavior as natural and temporary.

You can be enormously helpful by lending the parents a sympathetic ear and by reassuring them their feelings are normal. Restore their perspective by reminding them that children only

It's A Girl

demand 100 percent of their parents' attention for about three years. At that age, children can start preschool. Then, before you know it, most kids would rather memorize the *Iliad* than be seen with their parents. After that point, parents hear from their off-spring only when they need to borrow a car or bail money.

You can bolster the parents' self-confidence by compliment-ing them on the way they are handling the baby. If they need assistance in caring for your grandbaby, try to help without taking over or seeming so perfectly confident that you in-timidate the parents. Your goal should be to make them realize that they are already good parents and will become increasingly self-assured as they get to know their baby.

Usually postpartum depression sets in anywhere from a few days to a few weeks after the birth and lifts a few days after it begins. If your child has the blues more than two weeks or experiences a profound depression causing her to loose sleep, appetite, interest in her baby, her husband, and herself—call her doctor.

Your Grandbaby

Of course, your new grandbaby has his needs too. He has just made a radical transition from a dark, warm, wet environ-ment where his mother ate and breathed for him. Suddenly, he is rudely squeezed out into an arid, bright, noisy place with these big hairy things who seem to be interested in him. He doesn't know what he looks like, who he is, or exactly how he is separate from everything else.

What your grandbaby needs is time to collect himself. He requires lots of rest in a relatively quiet, warm place. When he is awake (which isn't often during the first couple of weeks), your grandbaby needs food (breast milk or formula), a clean diaper, and physical contact with a few loving adults.

One thing your grandbaby doesn't need is physical contact with a great many, although suitably admiring, people. Being handled by lots of visitors overstimulates and exhausts your grandbaby, and exposes him needlessly to germs. (Although the newborn immune system is immature, your grandbaby has ac-quired antibodies from the mother while still in the womb and from the mother's milk if he nurses. Your grandbaby, therefore, does carry some resistance to infectious diseases.)

You, the Grandparents

Fewer visitors during the first weeks also means more time for you to be with your grandbaby. Despite the fact that the literature is not flooded with articles on the significance of early grandparent-grandbaby bonding, intuition says that such contact is important.

As soon as you catch news of the birth, you are likely to be overwhelmed with an urge to see and touch your grandbaby. It is only natural that you should want to be with her. Just as with the parents, intimacy with your grandbaby strengthens your attachment and lays the foundation for future comradery.

If you can't be with your grandbaby immediately, remember that bonding occurs over an entire lifetime. The newborn period is not your only shot at forming a meaningful relationship with your grandchild.

Fortunately for you, some common parental reactions work to your advantage. A new mother usually feels that birth links her to every woman who ever lived, but especially to her own mother. Likewise, the father suddenly gains some insight into the experiences his own father might have had. For these reasons, new parents usually cannot wait to show off their little miracle to his grandparents. Given such an auspicious inauguration into grandparenthood, you should be able to satisfy your need to spend time with your grandbaby.

It may be difficult to help run a household that is not your own—particularly when you would rather nuzzle your grandbaby. Bear in mind that, with time, your role as a nurturer to your grandchildren will be fulfilled. As your first grandchild ages, the parents will have an easier time tearing themselves away and placing her in your care. Furthermore, if the parents produce more offspring, you will be needed to play with the older grandchildren, or to take care of a new grandbaby so that the parents can spend time with the older siblings.

Although there are many things you can do to help the parents and your grandchildren (and being needed is a wonderful thing), be sure to pay attention to signs of fatigue in yourself. If you allow yourself to become rundown or even sick, you won't be doing anyone a favor. Be sensible. If you have a bad back, don't lift older grandchildren or vacuum the house. If you have heart disease, don't offer to mow the lawn. If you actually hate to cook and clean, don't martyr yourself by volunteering to run the household. You are bound to communicate your disgruntled feelings to the parents. Do the things you feel comfortable doing and that *please* you.

If you behave courteously when a guest in the parents' home, give respectful consideration to the parents' need to be alone with their baby, and take care of yourself, your involvement in the celebration of your extending family should be fraught with delight. If tensions arise (as they often do whenever family members are in close quarters), open discussion of your feelings may go a long way in maintaining family harmony (and beats brandishing firearms).

Chapter Seven

FAMILY TIES

Or,
How You Can Drive Each Other Crazy

Somewhere between "To know me is to love me" and "Familiarity breeds contempt" lies the stuff of which familial bonds are made. Most young adults love their own parents deeply. When they are apart, these caring adults speak longingly, warmly of their parents. Yet, the aforementioned loving humans are driven to distraction within hours of being in the same household with their parents. When it comes time to separate again, they feel not only relief, but sadness that the precious time spent with their parents was not as harmonious as they had fantasized.

As you can attest, these schizophrenic feelings are shared by the older generation as well. Many a grandparent anticipated a joyous visit with children and grandchildren and departed feeling bewildered. Few situations are more painful than two generations coming together full of great expectations only to psychologically injure each other.

Here is a brief look at some of the many intergenerational bugaboos.

1. The Basic Generation Gap.

Given that you are totally unique, combined with the undeniable fact that you are older than your children, you are bound to disagree with at least one or two issues involving your grandchildren.

A common point of confusion arises from the paradox that many young parents are making use of highly technical medical developments, such as amniocentesis and ultrasound, at the same time that they are reverting to methods once considered outdated, such as birth without anesthesia and breast-feeding. Many child-rearing dogmas have shifted: when and what one feeds baby, when and how one potty trains baby, when and how one disciplines baby... All these issues and more are discussed in detail in other chapters.

Perhaps, after learning the rationale behind some of these modern ideas, your mind is flexible enough to accept them. You may not be irritated by the fact that your children are doing things differently. Unless, that is, they do what so many first-time parents do—proselytize. They take up a moral crusade: their ways against yours, modern ideology vs. the traditional tried and true. These zealots come armed to the battle with a battery of pamphlets, books, and quotes supporting their point of view. You might feel like granting them a point or two if they weren't so darned self-righteous.

How should you respond? If you want to put out the fire with gasoline, you can use the standard response, "We did thus and so, and you turned out all right. At least we thought you had until you started spouting such idiot drivel." What you are likely to get is an earful of statistics proving that your methods were misguided and downright dangerous.

If yours is a generous nature, you can smile to yourself and humor your children. If you find that you can be supportive of the philosophies your children have adopted, everyone will be happier. If you are troubled that they may be doing something potentially damaging to your grandchild, do your own research by reading or talking with an expert. You may need to express your divergent opinions—which leads to the next issue.

2. Unsolicited Advice.

Based upon your past experiences as a parent, you have no doubt come to many conclusions about right versus wrong ways to raise a child. You may hate to see your children make mistakes that could be avoided if only you enlightened them. Yet, at the same time, the image of yourself being the meddlesome, interfering grandparent is loathsome.

So, what is a concerned grandparent to do? Many times you will need to let the parents find their own way, just as you did when they were children. If something bothers you to the extent that you are suppressing negative feelings until they burst forth in an emotional froth, or if you are worried about your grandchild's welfare, find a friendly time to express your opinion in a nonthreatening, nonaccusing, unemotional fashion.

Keep in mind that few egos are as fragile as those of new parents. Parenting is a job no one wants to botch, making the recipient of the criticism all the more defensive. Even when your criticism is directed toward your grandchild, the parents will construe that you are finding fault with their parenting.

Parents love to hear how their superlative skills have produced veritable angels. A good trick (for those times when you feel you must pass on pearls of your wisdom) is to point out the good first. For example, "Ralphie, you folded that diaper masterfully. However, I think it would work better if you put it on the other end."

Whenever you feel compelled to make suggestions (a euphemism for advice), remember your own experiences with your parents and in-laws when you were raising your children. You may have felt resentment at being the recipient of relentless criticism and advice. If you can admit that you made some mistakes, you can accept that your children are going to make their own errors. Furthermore, remind yourself that your children are now the ones in charge. Unless you actually do spend more time with your grandchild than the parents do, they will resent any intimations that you understand him better. You can proffer your advice, but the parents have the right to reject it. If, at this point, you cannot go along with their viewpoint, it may be time to seek professional counseling.

As always, the sword cuts both ways. You may find yourself being on the receiving end of criticism. Some parents have the impression that no one else can care for their children as well as they themselves can. Any variation from their routine is nothing short of wrong.

Because you have the dubious honor of being family, your children may be more likely to open their ungrateful mouths to you than to a hired baby-sitter. Instead of thanking you for so generously spending your Saturday night changing diapers, your child may instead point out every minutia that ran counter to The Routine, such as giving Junior his bath before instead of after dinner.

Your rebuttal will be tempered by your past patterns. Try to avoid verbal warfare. Withdraw from the battlefield and wait for a more relaxed time to discuss what seemed to be hurtful or unwarranted criticism. Later, remind the parents that it is impossible for you to do everything exactly as they do when you are caring for your grandbaby. Tell the parents that if they don't want you to criticize them, you expect the same courtesy.

3. Solicited Advice.

What if your children have the good sense to seek your advice? Then, you should still strive to be tactful, to slip in a compliment or two along with any constructive criticisms you have.

What if, on the other hand, your children disappoint you by seldom asking your opinion? In the old days, parents learned most of what they needed to know from the older generation. Now, parents are more likely to turn to books, health care professionals, and fellow parents than to their own parents.

Why this change? One reason is geographical separation. A new mother may be unwilling to make a long distance phone call just to ask her mother what brand of baby cereal she recommends.

A more important reason is the burgeoning of medical information over the past several years. Unless you have advanced training in pediatrics, your children are liable to write you off as insufficiently informed about modern parenting. Perhaps people tend to overintellectualize things these days.

Whether or not your children actively seek your guidance, you can be sure they will be influenced by the way you raised them. It is what is most familiar to them. Although they may not realize it, your children will imitate your parenting techniques in many ways.

4. Breaking Rules.

When you come to your grandchild's home, try to respect the rules and routines the parents have worked hard to establish. The Important Rules usually center around food and eating behavior, sleep habits, discipline techniques, and television viewing.

For example, you have been told by the earnest new parents that they are striving to keep the word "chocolate" out of Missy's vocabulary, not to mention her mouth. You are also savvy enough to know that this is a realistic aspiration only so long as Missy never sees a television commercial and never goes to school, the grocery store, or anyone else's home. So, you decide to come for a visit laden with all manner of chocolate decadence. Don't expect a thank-you note. The parents of this now hyper, chocolate-addicted little fiend may not appreciate your insight.

Likewise, when your grandchild comes to your home for a visit, the parents need to respect your requests. Ideally, you will be able to accommodate them on the Major Rules. However, you may have your own house rules. For example, Missy can follow her usual dietary regime of yogurt, tofu, and granola. She must,

91

however, confine her meals to the kitchen rather than spread food remnants about your home.

If you are going to baby-sit your grandchild, keeping to the regular routine will help both the child and the parents. Your grandchild will have a smoother transition to your care if the new schedule resembles the usual routine. Her parents will feel happier when they return if they do not have to spend a month undoing the "objectionable" habits you have created.

This is not to say that you should be expected to be a carbon copy of the parents. Your grandchild loves you because you are you. You look, smell, talk, walk, laugh, and play delightfully differently. You should be allowed to establish your own relationship with your grandchildren. Parents who expect you to do every little thing in *exactly* the same fashion they do are being unreasonable. Besides, children are flexible, and having some variety in their little lives keeps them so.

A corollary of breaking the rules is overindulging your grandchild. If you are taking care of your precious grandchild for a time and cater to her every whim in a way the parents either can't or won't imitate, then you are doing everyone a disservice. After you are out of the picture, the parents may be left in charge of a clingy, demanding, whining child until they regain control.

One aspect of overindulgence involves lavish gift giving. You may idealize that grandparents should resemble (in spirit) a certain jolly, round, white-haired individual clad in red. If you enjoy giving gifts, you should. But bear in mind that, although a child does not become spoiled just because she owns many things, she may become accustomed to being showered with trinkets. (A child may also become overwhelmed if you give her too many playthings all at once.) If you routinely give your grandchild gifts upon greeting her, she may also come to regard a present as your toll for admission ("Great to see you Gramps! But, where's my loot?"). Furthermore, the parents will cringe when they walk in the front door and receive the salutation, "Well, where are my presents?"

Don't lose sight of the fact that you can give to your grandchildren in many invaluable and diverse ways that do not involve spending sums rivaling the federal deficit. Just taking the time to visit represents an invaluable gift. You can also treat your grandchild to an outing, share your hobbies and interests, mend their broken toys or torn clothing, check out library books for them, pass on family keepsakes, songs, recipes, stories....

5. The Issue of Permissiveness.
Some grandparents feel that today's parents are more permissive than their generation was. Permissiveness is really a relative thing. Parents and grandparents may have different thresholds for when they "lower the boom." Also, the two generations may have established different priority lists for what constitutes misbehavior.

For instance, because the Clean Plate Club has failed to alleviate Third World hunger and has contributed to a number of cases of obesity, many parents now allow their children to leave food on their plates. Yet, the parents may limit sweets more than the grandparents would.

Another example is the issue of exploration. Parents now are more likely to permit their children full range of the household, preferring to move breakables to saying NO! a thousand times. Or, they may allow their toddler to touch the control panel of the television, but a grandparent might consider such tampering strictly off limits. On the other hand, parents might be more restrictive of television viewing.

If you two older generations disagree on certain issues, discuss the problem calmly and try to respect each other's wishes in each other's households.

6. The Hovering Eager Beaver.
There may be times, especially with the arrival of the first grandchild, when you will swear that your children have forgotten than you are also a parent. Or, maybe they are concerned that because it's been such a long time since you tended small children, you must have forgotten the basics and that you can recall is hopelessly outdated.

Hence, these anxious parents may hang over your shoulder as you gently, competently scoop up your grandbaby and exclaim, "Don't drop her!" You might be tempted to reply, "Oh, come on. Can't I just drop her once?"

When you baby-sit for the first time, you may have to endure a blow-by-blow account of every little thing you should do for your grandbaby. After the parents depart, you can park yourself next to the telephone until you field the first half-dozen phone calls from them. By then, they should feel reassured that "everything is all right" and it is probably safe for you to take your grandbaby for a stroll.

On the other side of this coin is the unnervingly competent grandparent (usually the female variety) who marches in and announces to the new parents that she has arrived "to take over." Now this grandparent may really mean, "I've come to help you, to give you a rest. Tell me how I can be useful." If, however, the grandparent attempts to assume all baby care responsibilities (as opposed to other domestic duties), conflict is inevitable. First-time parents often can't get enough of their newborn. They need plenty of time being the primary caretakers to gain the confidence essential to successful parenting.

The irritations of the hovering parent and the overly eager grandparent usually are most problematic with the first grandchild and abate with time. When the parents see that you can be trusted with their precious cargo, they will (hopefully) stop hovering. Soon, they will yearn for a romantic dinner for two and beg you to baby-sit. When the parents have produced another grandchild, they will be incredibly grateful for any help they can get. Also, your energies will be diffused when you have more grandchildren to love.

7. Too Much or Too Little of a Good Thing.

After the parents have oversaturated their need to cuddle their little darling, they may begin to equate you with the archetypal, perfect baby-sitter. If you live nearby, you may start to feel overly popular. The parents may have the mistaken notion that your life is a void to be filled with baby-sitting your grandchildren. If you are a person who has difficulty saying no, you might experience second parenthood.

Before all hopes of taking that month-long Caribbean cruise fade (and, in fact, your children are taking that cruise and leaving you behind to baby-sit), declare your rights. Find a casual time to sit down with the parents and let them know how often you are willing to baby-sit. They won't know until you tell them.

But, what if the problem is the reverse? What if you yearn to see your grandchildren and do so only infrequently? Chapter eight discusses potential impediments to a close relationship with your grandchildren and offers a few solutions.

This chapter has listed some of the possible sources of irritation between parents and grandparents. Every relationship is unique and creates its own blend of harmony and discord. Conflicts are virtually inescapable in close relationships. But because most people need love, it is better to learn to solve problems than to avoid human contact. Your relationship with your family is not measured by the number of ways you disagree, but by the manner in which you resolve your disagreements.

Chapter Eight

CHANGING ROLES

Mothers' Expanded New Role

In the old days, a "well-bred" woman was expected to be educated sufficiently to cook, clean, sew, entertain guests, write social correspondence, and play a musical instrument. Then, her mission in life was to marry, have babies, and put to use the above mentioned skills whilst the nanny took care of the children.

Scarlet O'Hara, roll over. Now, women's horizons have broadened. Much like men, women can do almost anything they put their minds to. In fact, women are expected to accomplish more than men during their lifetimes.

The Contemporary Woman is supposed to graduate from college, attend business school, become a famous investment banker, marry, and drop a baby or two—without missing a step in the corporate beat. Furthermore, she should know how to prepare gourmet meals, run an immaculate household that should be featured at least once in *Architectural Digest*, sew, entertain guests, write brilliant social correspondence, and play a musical instrument in the local symphony. Yes, Contemporary Woman can "have it all," including the nervous breakdown.

When Contemporary Woman finds herself to be "with child," she faces a dilemma: to work or not to work or to work part-time. If a woman wants to or must return to work full-time after a short maternity leave, she will be accused of child neglect by at least half the population, some of whom are women who have stayed home with children and really hated it. If a woman decides to put her career on hold to be home with her children, she will be scorned by the other half of the population, some of whom are working women who (secretly) wish they were home raising children.

So, Contemporary Woman can choose one of three routes:

1) She can brave vicious criticism to stay at home full-time.

2) She can brave vicious criticism to work outside the home full-time.

3) Hedging her bets, she can endure only mild disapproval by taking the middle-of-the-road approach and work part-time outside the home and the rest of the time inside the home.

Statistics show that more than 60 percent of mothers with children under 14 work outside the home. Many of these women go back to work well before their children's first birthday.

Why do so many mothers work outside the home?

They enjoy their jobs.

They need the money.

Their mothers didn't.

Their mothers did.

They quickly realize it is easier than taking care of a household of small children.

A combination of the above.

The sad reality is that 70 percent of mothers work because of economic necessity. Unfortunately, the United States is the only Western nation that does not require employers to guarantee maternity leave. Most new mothers are stuck with two options: settling for a short (often unpaid) maternity leave or losing their jobs in order to stay home longer with their babies.

Contrast this data about the soaring number of working mothers with the abysmal state of child care. As you are probably well aware, the extended family is an endangered species. Many grandparents live far away or are out there holding down jobs themselves instead of baking pies in their cozy homes over the river and through the woods. Most working mothers don't have the luxury of entrusting the care of their children to loving grandparents, aunts, or uncles.

No, Contemporary Woman must search for a reasonable facsimile of child care—often beginning her quest before the birth. She can either enroll her child in a day-care center, take her child to another mother's home, hire a sitter to come to her home while she works, or find a live-in nanny.

Most parents wish for a Mary Poppins—someone who will love their children and teach them all kinds of wonderful things; someone who is kind, attractive, intelligent, creative, industrious, and reliable. The reality is that most people who possess these personal attributes realize they could earn a lot more money practicing law than baby-sitting. If they allow themselves to be hired as a sitter in the first place, they generally last at best a few months before moving on to greener salaries.

Quality child care is not only scarce but often expensive. A woman can easily spend a substantial hunk of her salary on child care. Finding a reliable, affordable parent surrogate has become an extremely stressful obstacle for working parents today. What is the solution? As a humanitarian gesture, Congress could pass legislation that would effectively double the salary of one parent so that the other could stay home with the children, the governess, the butler, the cook, and several maids. A more realistic solution would be for government or private businesses or both to subsidize affordable, readily available child care. A fairy-tale solution would be for all grandparents either to quit their jobs or to come out of retirement and then move to their grandchildren's neighborhood to better entertain them.

Fathers' Expanded New Role

In the old days, a man was expected to be educated sufficiently to read and comprehend *Sports Illustrated* and to find a suitable job. Then, he was free to find a mate, marry, procreate, and bring home the proverbial bacon.

Contemporary Man can do these things and much more. Social pressures now dictate that he attend prepared childbirth classes, "mother" his wife during her pregnancy, participate actively in the birth of his babies, change diapers, and go to P.T.A. meetings.

Rumor has it that the Contemporary Man is much more magnanimous about offering to baby-sit the kids while his wife takes a much-needed break to do something self-indulgent like grocery shop for the household. This is indeed a small step forward.

The reason it is not a large step forward is that having Daddy baby-sit is not the same as having Grandma or even the twelve-year-old neighbor baby-sit. Men often interpret baby-sitting quite narrowly. Mom should not be surprised to walk in the door with armloads of groceries to find the breakfast dishes still on the table; the kids (still in their pajamas and the same diaper she last changed) out stomping in mud puddles; and good old Dad ensconced in an armchair, beer in one hand, bowl of popcorn in the other, blissfully watching Wimbledon. He may not understand that other duties are expected other than glancing over his shoulder at his brood every hour or so. Today's mother must learn to exert supreme self-control to prevent herself from shooting her mate when he grins and casually remarks, "Hey, honey, taking care of the kids is a breeze!"

But, seriously, men are now given much more encouragement—from psychologists, the media, their peers, and their wives—to involve themselves with the direct, hands-on business of raising their children. Active, compassionate fathering is beneficial for both the children and the father. Children clearly prosper from the presence of a loving father. Daddy usually plays with the kids differently than Mommy (more rambunctiously, especially during the half-hour before bedtime). The father figure gives a little boy a very important role model and a little girl the gold standard to which other men are later compared. And for the man who takes the time to really know his children, he earns the priceless treasure of his youngsters' love and admiration.

Grandparents' New Role

In the introduction to this book, you read that compared to previous generations today's grandparents are healthier, wealthier, enjoy more leisure time, and have fewer grandchildren.

Furthermore, you grandparents have the advantages of telephone communication and air travel to keep you in touch with distant family members. Putting all these factors together yields a generation of grandparents who can orchestrate a close relationship with each grandchild.

You may be wondering, "But, didn't grandparents spend more time with their grandchildren back in the days of the extended family?" Not really. It is true that, before the turn of this century, grandparents often lived in the same household with the younger generations. That grandparents lived with their grandchildren is mostly myth. Grandparents usually shared a home with their *un*married children. If a grandparent moved in with a married child, she was usually a widow. Furthermore, grandchildren far outnumbered grandparents, leaving a small percentage of grandchildren who actually lived with their grandparents.

Now, most grandparents are likely to live independently of their adult children. Furthermore, most senior citizens are proud of their independence and would not willingly give it up —even for the pleasure of seeing much more of their grandchildren. You've paid your dues, right? You have perhaps been hoping that you would live to see the day when you again had your house to yourself, when you didn't have to suffer inner ear damage while your teenaged children played their favorite rock and roll albums?

But, if you live in a different house, not to mention a different state, from your grandchildren, what kind of a role can you play as a grandparent? Is grandparenthood a marginal, honorific title? It doesn't have to be.

Playing the part of grandparent has become much more fun. As a whole, your counterparts of the previous generation had a stiffer, more formal style. Granted, they may have garnered more respect from their grandchildren. But as Contemporary Grandparents who adopt a warmer, friendlier relationship with your grandchildren, you stand to gain much more in the way of emotional fulfillment. The flow of emotional current moves both directions. If you have a loving relationship with your grandchildren, you will be rewarded with babbling phone calls, illegible letters, and crudely made place mats.

Although you can largely abandon the rather repugnant role of authority figure to the middle generation, situations might arise making it necessary for you to act as a surrogate parent to your grandchildren. One of the very important functions of grandparents is that of reserve core or shock absorbers for the family. In times of crisis—separation, divorce, illness, death—

you may be needed to care for your grandchildren, to give them a sense of stability. In the absence of a catastrophic event, you may be asked to take care of your grandchildren while the parents take a much-needed vacation (and thus avert a family crisis).

Because your relationship with your grandchildren is largely devoid of the weighty responsibilities of parenthood, you can create a magical relationship with your grandchildren. You embody the venerable protagonists of childhood lore—the Fairy Godmother, Merlin, the Good Witch, and the Wizard of Oz. You have the chance to be a weaver of fabulous tales, a composer of silly songs, and a personal friend of the fairies, elves, and Santa Claus.

Aside from your roles as nurturer, caretaker, and family magician, you are also a teacher and historian. Your personal vignettes provide your grandchildren with fascinating information about what life was like before the availability of home video recorders. If you share your hobbies and favorite pastimes with your grandchildren, they stand to learn about things their parents either don't do or don't have the time to do. When you pass on family rituals, you give your grandchildren a sense of tradition.

Without conscious effort, you will provide your grandchildren with a role model of grandparenthood. When your grandchildren are themselves grandparents, they will think back to the things you did together and perhaps recreate some of those treasured moments.

Furthermore, your grandchildren will learn from you what it means to grow old. If you have a positive attitude about aging, your grandchildren will more likely be optimistic about their own old age. If you have a good relationship with your grandchildren, they will transfer their specific affection for you to a more general feeling of good will toward all elderly people.

From the parents' point of view, your role may be that of confidant, expert on child rearing, most valuable baby-sitter, and loan officer. How do you get yourself in shape for these tasks?

- ☐ You can sharpen your listening skills and remind yourself to give advice only when asked (and then, with extreme tact).

☐ You can share your own experiences of bringing up children and, at the same time, remain open to the different theories the parents have heard or read.

☐ You can avoid future conflict by establishing your baby-sitting limits early in the game.

☐ You can avert intergenerational embarrassment by making clear your relative willingness to provide financial support.

Potential Impediments to the Blissful Fulfillment of Your Grandparental Roles:

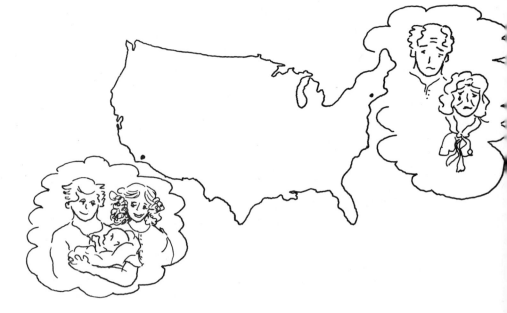

1) The number-one enemy of grandparents who want to spend a lot of time with their grandchildren is *geographical separation*. A recent study demonstrated that grandparents who live less than a mile from their grandchildren can expect an average of 102 visits per year. When grandparents and grandchildren are separated by more than 100 miles, the number of visits per year drops to three. This data gains further relevance when you consider that the frequency of your visits with your grandchildren is the most important ingredient for fostering a close relationship with them.

2) Another roadblock is placed in the path of your grandparenting career if you get along poorly with the mother. Mothers are more likely than fathers to control who visits with their children and when.

3) The age of your grandchildren greatly influences the intensity of your relationship. Grandparents tend to have stronger ties with their preadolescent grandchildren. Teenagers tend to busy themselves with school, work, and especially with their peers (no doubt, doing things of which you don't approve).

4) The expanded role of fathers in child rearing should not threaten or supplant your role as grandparents. However, you grandmothers may feel particularly annoyed if you perceive that between *two* doting parents you'll never have a chance to be alone with your grandchild.

If you feel as though the father has usurped your rightful role, you are probably dealing with a *new* father. If so, take heart. Typically, new fathers are most zealous about their involvement with their children during the newborn period. Lucky for you, very few companies offer fathers extended paternity leave. Besides, as time goes by, the "new" will wear off and the parents will long to get away and leave you with your grandchild. Furthermore, with each subsequent grandbaby, you will be even more needed.

5) One last potential obstacle between you and your grandchildren is competition with the other grandparents. Ideally, you have a fantastic relationship with all your in-laws and don't worry about who sees whom more, who gives jazzier gifts to whom, who loves whom the best.... However, if the other grandparents live closer to your grandchildren, reside in a more alluring location, or are on friendlier terms with the parents, you

may indeed see relatively less of your grandchildren. If you feel resentment about getting short shrift, you will need to speak to your children about finding ways to bring you together with your extended family more often.

Ways to Maximize Your Career as a Grandparent:

1) Because geographical separation is one of the most formidable obstacles in the quest to be connected to one's grandchildren, the obvious solution would seem to be to move to the same neighborhood. Before you do that, you may need to consider things such as whether you really want to give up your condominium in sunny Leisure World and move to snowy North Dakota; whether you can leave the security of friends; whether you could afford the expense of moving; and whether you will get along well with the middle generation in a situation when you will see them frequently. Obviously, this is a decision that shouldn't be made without an intergenerational powwow.

2) A less-dramatic solution is to minimize the effects of distance by traveling frequently. Many airlines offer special memberships with reduced rates for senior citizens. Once again, you need to work out with your family how long and where you can comfortably stay. Rather than always passively waiting to be summoned by the parents, take the initiative to invite your family to visit you. You can also sponsor family vacations. These reunions can generate the kinds of memories (of the mosquito-infested camping trip, the flat tire outside of Rifle, Colorado...) that knit a family closer together.

3) When travel isn't feasible, you can fortify family ties by communicating frequently with your children and grandchildren. You can write, telephone, send photographs of yourself, make audio tapes of yourself talking. All of these things will keep you in the minds of your grandchildren. Your efforts to stay in touch can also strengthen your relationships with your adult children. And, if you have a good rapport with the parents, they are more likely to make an effort to bring you together with your grandchildren.

4) Another way to keep yourself in the minds of your children and grandchildren is to hand down family recipes,

jokes, stories, songs, and rituals (such as making one piece of quilt for each family member's birthday). For years to come, your grandchildren will think of you every time they eat Gram's eggplant casserole, hear the story of Grampa falling off the horse, repeat Granddaddy's Nixon jokes, sing Nanny's French nursery rhymes....

5) Lastly, try to stay on good terms with the parents, the gatekeepers to your grandchildren. Endear yourself to the middle generation by being emotionally supportive—listening to their problems, offering suggestions when your advice is solicited, biting your tongue when unwarranted criticisms bubble into the speech center of your brain, and, in general, behaving as you would toward any good friend. You can also be helpful in very practical ways such as baby-sitting (if you enjoy it) or loaning the family money (if you can afford to do so). If you are invited to visit, remember that you are a guest and try to be a considerate one.

Things that go around usually come around. And in this instance, your fine efforts may be reciprocated by the parents. When frictions do arise, discuss them in an open, honest, and friendly fashion (being sure to lock the cutlery safely away first). If you find that despite your noblest efforts you cannot get along with the parents, professional counselling is one avenue toward healing your relationship.

Things That Work to Your Advantage Toward an Intimate Grandparent-Grandchild Relationship

Lest this chapter end leaving you with the impression that you have to fight an uphill battle to develop a close relationship with your grandchildren, consider the many factors that you already have going for you:

1) Most parents are just big children who still want to win their parents' approval. Your adult children will want you to adore your grandchildren because it makes them feel as though they have done something grand in your eyes. They will naturally want to share these little marvels with you. If you offer the

younger generations warm approval, love, and encouragement, they will keep coming back for more.

2) Your strongest advantages are inherent to the grandparent-grandchild relationship. The old and the very young have many things in common. Even before they retire, many senior citizens have slowed the pace of their life-styles. Small children are protected by labor law from employment. Both generations, therefore, enjoy more leisure time than the middle generation. Both generations are enough outside the bustle of the workaday world to open all sensory modalities to the world of wonder. The parents are under more pressure to "do things" and have less time to smell the roses, collect rocks, examine ant colonies, and leave notes for the wood sprites. Your grandchildren will appreciate your less hurried style, your capacity just to be with them.

3) Children are just naturally drawn to old people. Because you are a grandparent, you are wise and experienced in the eyes of a small child. You are the voice of times past. And the fascination runs in reverse too: older people gravitate toward those delightful wee ones.

4) Furthermore, because of your experience as a parent, you have learned something about the way children *really* are. Now that you are a grandparent, you can let go of notions of the way children should be. The members of the middle generation get caught up in learning how to be a "good parents" who will raise "good children." Because you probably have fewer expectations of your grandchildren than do their parents, your relationship contains less tension. You exude a sense of easygoing affection, of love regardless of batting averages and penmanship marks. Your grandchildren need your affirmation of their inherent goodness.

Lastly, if you don't live with your grandchildren, your visits will be viewed as special treats. Your grandchildren will treasure the things you do together, in part because the time is so precious.

Chapter Nine

REINTRODUCING THE NEWBORN

Hello, Grandbaby!

If you are a grandparent, you must have, at one time in your life, seen a newborn baby. Ah, but how quickly one forgets the unique features of the freshly born—the way they look, feel, smell; the things they can and cannot do. This chapter provides you with a brief refresher course.

General Physical Appearance

Your newly born grandbaby looks quite different from the older baby. Her head is relatively huge, measuring one fourth of her entire length. Her munchkin legs are disproportionately short, constituting only one-third of her length. Clearly, athletic skills take a back seat to brain growth during fetal development.

The Head

On closer inspection of your grandbaby's head, other peculiarities are evident. Take, for instance, the shape. You may wonder whether your grandbaby inherited this cone-shaped head from someone on the *other* side of the family. Probably not.

Your grandbaby's head was *temporarily* and *reversibly* molded into this unusual shape as it squeezed through the birth canal. Molding is possible because the separate plates of bone that make up the skull do not fuse for many months. In fact, as you gently caress the top of her head, you can feel areas where the bones do not even touch. These soft spots, or *fontanels*, will close by 18 months. Don't worry about harming your grandbaby by gently touching these areas. The underlying brain is still covered by the scalp and tough membranes.

Eyes

Your grandbaby's eyelids may appear a bit red and swollen from pressure exerted on them during the delivery. Additionally, the routine use of antibiotic eye drops can cause temporary irritation. Your grandbaby will not necessarily look beady-eyed in the future.

As your new grandchild studies your face, don't be alarmed if both eyes do not move perfectly in concert. The muscles that move the eyes are still a little weak at birth. Unless one eye is fixed in its deviation, such wandering is normal and will correct itself.

Ears

At birth, the cartilage in the outer ear is still soft and flexible. If an ear appears to be folded, don't worry; it will probably straighten on its own accord. "Pinning" the ear to the side of the head with tape (or holding it back with your fingers) is neither necessary nor recommended.

Nose and Mouth

At the time of delivery, your grandbaby's nose and mouth probably contained a little mucous, which was cleared using a bulb syringe. A tissue or a clean bulb syringe can be (gently) used over the next weeks if the nose is congested. Your grandbaby may clear her nose herself by sneezing. Thus, sneezing is not always the harbinger of a cold.

An occasional newborn already has a tooth or two. If they are loose, the doctor may extract them to prevent choking.

Skin

The average baby's skin is astonishingly soft, seamless, and toned. This phenomenon becomes more remarkable as the age of the observer increases. However, your grandbaby's skin may not be altogether flawless, especially for the first few weeks.

Overall, a newborn's skin has a ruddy hue. Because the circulation is not completely mature the first few days, the hands and feet may appear to be tinged with blue.

If your grandbaby did a lot of sucking in the womb, he may have blisters on his lips, hands, or forearms.

Birthmarks are fairly common. Babies of darker-skinned parents may have "Mongolian spots," which are due to a bluish pigmentation under the skin over the low back and buttocks. "Stork bites" or "angel kisses" are red, flat birthmarks usually located on the bridge of the nose, upper eyelids, or back of the neck. They commonly disappear by the second birthday, but may reappear briefly with crying.

Descent through the birth canal probably is no pleasure cruise for the infant. Bruising about the head is one manifestation of a rough ride, especially after a forceps delivery. Like all bruises, these skin discolorations will fade. However, bruising does increase the likelihood that the baby will develop jaundice. Jaundice, a yellow cast to the skin and whites of the eyes, is common among newborns. It is usually caused by an immaturity in the liver's ability to clear the by-products of old blood cells. In most babies, jaundice resolves spontaneously within a few weeks.

Another variation from the ideal peaches-and-cream complexion is garden-variety newborn rashes. These blemishes often develop within the first few days of life, are usually harmless, and go away on their own. One of the things that may besmirch baby's face are milia, or tiny white pimples, caused by maternal hormones. Another common infant rash has a more cumbersome name, erythema toxicum, a collection of red bumps with yellow centers that give the baby the appearance of having been bitten by fleas. It, too, is harmless and disappears in a week or two without any treatment.

Peeling skin is also a common feature of the newborn. After the birth, peeling is most noticeable on the palms and soles, as though the baby developed dishpan hands and feet after spending nine months in her aqueous environment. In babies born later than the expected 40 weeks, peeling is more exuberant. A flaky scurf known as "cradle cap" is often present on the scalp. This flaking goes away on its own, and applications of oils and ointments are totally unnecessary.

The Chest

Your new grandbaby breathes about three or four times faster than you at a rate of 30 to 50 times a minute. Furthermore, the rate is often irregular. His pulse is also relatively rapid, ranging between 130 and 160 beats per minute.

Exposure to the high levels of maternal hormones during fetal development cause the breasts (of both boy and girl babies) to be somewhat enlarged at birth. Rarely, the breasts may even excrete a few drops of milk ("witches milk"). Rest assured that, contrary to the lore of old, such a baby is *not* bewitched. The breasts should be left alone. When the hormone levels fall, breasts will decrease in size and cease to produce milk.

The Genitals

The mother's hormones also cause your grandbaby's genitals to appear swollen at birth. This is especially true for girls, who may also have a small amount of blood-tinged vaginal discharge in the first weeks of life due to withdrawal from these hormones.

Boys come equipped with a penis complete with protective foreskin. (See Chapter six for information on circumcision. See Chapter ten for genital hygiene.)

The Abdomen

Many an older sibling, who has accepted all the other little peculiarities of the new brother or sister, balks at "that yucky thing hanging out of the belly button." You, of course, will recall that after the umbilical cord is cut, a stump remains. If kept clean and dry (see Chapter ten), this remnant of the cord will fall off within a couple of weeks.

Your grandbaby's first bowel movements will consist of a sticky greenish-black substance called *meconium*. After a few days, a breast-fed baby's stools will appear yellow and some-

117

what loose. If bottle-fed, your grandbaby's stools will be browner and firmer.

The Extremities

Your newly born grandbaby might put you in mind of a frog by the way her legs flop open at the hips. In general, new babies keep their arms and legs flexed close to their bodies. For months, the hands are primarily held in tight fists.

The Hair

Babies are born with varying amounts of hair on their pointy heads. Most of this hair will fall out and be replaced by hair that is quite different in color and texture. Body hair or *lanugo* may be visible especially in the form of some downy fuzz on the back. If your grandbaby arrived prematurely, he will have more lanugo. Body hair disappears over the next few weeks.

A Review of Newborn Reflexes

For your grandbaby, birth marks a dramatic transition from languishing in a watery environment where all her basic needs were passively met to an arid place where she must breathe, eat, and effectively communicate her needs to older, more capable, obliging humans. Fortunately, your grandbaby comes equipped with all kinds of reflexes (summarized in the following table) to help maximize her success until she is experienced enough to do these things herself.

Sensory Perception: The Touchy-feely Stuff

For the present generation of parents and grandparents, much new information is available regarding the maturity at birth of the five senses: touch, smell, taste, hearing, and vision. Babies perceive much more than people used to suspect. Fortunately, however, for some time to come, they remain fairly uncritical observers. Wrinkles, balding, acne, a crooked nose—to the infant these are just interesting variations of the human visage.

Knowing what babies perceive allows parents and grandparents to appropriately stimulate and thus help complete the maturation of the senses. Failure to stimulate a baby's senses

Table of Newborn Reflexes

ROOTING REFLEX	Stimulation of the cheek, mouth, or lips causes your grandbaby's head to turn toward the stimulus (e.g., nipple), her mouth to open, and her tongue to come forward. This reflex helps your grandbaby find the breast or bottle.
SWALLOW REFLEX	Stimulation of the inside of the mouth causes automatic sucking and swallowing.
HAND-TO-MOUTH REFLEX	Stroking your grandbaby's cheek or palm causes her mouth to "root" (turn toward the stimulus) and her arm to flex. After hand and mouth find each other, vigorous sucking follows.
RIGHTING REFLEX	Your grandbaby attempts to pull her head to an upright position when pulled to a sit.
TONIC NECK REFLEX	When lying supine with head turned to the side, his arm on this side straightens and the opposite arm bends resembling the "fencing position."
GRASPING REFLEX	Placing a finger in your grandbaby's palm or on the sole of her foot causes her fingers or toes to curl downward.
STEPPING REFLEX	Holding your grandbaby upright and pressing the sole of one foot at a time to a firm surface causes the alternate leg to bend as though walking.
MORO OR STARTLE REFLEX	A loud noise or rough handling causes your grandbaby to throw back her arms and legs, extend the neck, and cry out. Afterwards, her arms are brought together in an embrace and her legs flex.

can have deleterious effects on his future development. Fortunately, most folks instinctively give a baby what he needs.

Touch

Babies are very sensual creatures. An acute sense of touch is well developed long before birth. Inside the womb, the fetus feels the amniotic fluid slosh over his skin, his mother's hands feeling for his kicking feet, and a rocking motion as his mother moves through space. After the birth, similar sensations are comforting to the infant—being held snugly, rocked gently, and massaged.

Seemingly mundane activities—changing your grandbaby's clothes, bathing him, feeding him, rubbing his back, walking with him in your arms—all are effective means of stimulating his sense of touch and movement. If you want to know more, there are books, magazines, and classes on infant massage and exercises available in most communities.

Smell and Taste

Your grandbaby is born with the ability to keenly discriminate odors. He quickly learns to recognize the characteristic scent of familiar people. Although his taste buds are not entirely mature, your grandbaby can discern sweet from sour, and, not surprisingly, prefers the former.

Hearing

Months before birth, your grandbaby can hear. Because she has grown accustomed to listening to her mother's heartbeat,

your grandbaby is soothed by being held next to your chest where she can hear a similar rhythm.

Most babies prefer higher-pitched voices. Instinct seems to prompt people to talk like Minnie Mouse when they speak to an infant.

It doesn't require a Ph.D. in infant development to conclude that loud, sharp noises often upset babies. The corollary is that soft, rhythmical sounds are soothing to babies. Music boxes, toys that play songs, soft music on the stereo, a musical instrument, or your own voice will all entertain your grandbaby and stimulate his hearing.

Vision

Not many years ago, many people thought babies were blind at birth. The news is that your grandbaby can see *before* birth. Granted, the womb does not provide an exciting palette of color and form. If the mother had the luxury of exposing her belly to bright sunlight, your grandbaby's prebirth world was dimly illuminated. Otherwise, it was a very dark place.

The newborn's eye has been likened to an old-fashioned, fixed-focus camera. She is not able to adjust her eyes to clearly focus on images closer than eight inches nor farther than ten inches away. The ability to accommodate (focus the eyes with changing object distance) matures by four months. At this age, your grandbaby not only sees distant objects clearly, but focuses better than does the average adult on images that are very close.

As previously described, at birth, the muscles that move the eyes are somewhat lacking in strength and coordination. It is not uncommon, for one eye to drift occasionally. As long as one eye is not fixed in its deviation, such wandering is normal. Within a month or two, the eyes should move smoothly in concert as they follow an object. Maturation of the eye muscles is essential for the development of depth perception. Before two months of age, your grandbaby will probably have little appreciation of depth. Relative distances will be discerned by four to six months. The experience of reaching and crawling is needed before your grandbaby really understands the significance of heights. Before this time, she will probably roll fearlessly over the edge of anything. The newborn's lack of good judgment about the environment is one of the reasons for the admonition "never leave a child unattended."

Color vision is immature at birth. It starts to develop between 10 and 12 weeks. By four months of age, infants see all colors well and often prefer red.

What does your grandbaby like to watch? At birth, most babies prefer objects that offer a high contrast. At first, they prefer black and white geometric patterns of stripes and angles. Later, they prefer circular patterns such as a target or bull's eye. Much later, they prefer expensive objects like diamonds and sports cars.

You may notice that some mobiles on the market have an array of black and white geometrically patterned squares. To you, this type of mobile is far less appealing than a mobile hung with pastel-colored zoo animals. To your grandchild, this colorless mobile full of contrasting lines is actually quite stimulating.

Within the first three weeks of life, the most exciting image in your grandbaby's visual field becomes none other than the human face. Because hairlines and eyes offer the most contrast, you may notice that your grandbaby spends most of her time scanning the top half of your face. By three months of age, she will have learned to recognize familiar faces.

During the first two months of life while your grandbaby is getting herself organized, visual stimuli should be kept fairly low keyed. A bombardment of jazzy mobiles and flashy toys will only distract your grandbaby from important developmental tasks and may even make her jittery and upset.

122

By four months of age, the entire visual system has completely matured. Your grandbaby will now enjoy objects that are colorful, novel, complex, and in motion. By this time, your grandbaby will have gained considerable control over her head and hand movements and will be ready to explore her visual environment. You can stimulate her development by surrounding her with a manageable number of safe, interesting objects.

Growth

A basic principle of child development is that children increase in size. Actually, the most rapid growth occurs within the womb.

The average full-term newborn weighs roughly 7½ pounds (3.4 kilograms). Most newborns weigh between 5½ and 10 pounds. The average length is 20 inches (50 centimeters) and ranges between 18 and 22 inches. The head circumference averages 14 inches (35 centimeters).

Your grandbaby (whether breast-fed or bottle-fed) will probably lose from six to ten percent of his original birth weight during the first few days after birth. Most of this weight reduction represents a loss of excess body water. After three or four days, he will begin to regain this weight. By 10 to 14 days of age, he should have reattained or surpassed his birth weight.

During the ensuing three months, your grandbaby will grow at an incredible pace, gaining nearly an ounce a day. Between three and six months, his rate of weight gain will decrease slightly to four or five ounces a week. The second half of the first year, the weight gain tapers to a mere two to three ounces a week. Thankfully, his growth rate will slack off to a relatively slow and steady rate for the remainder of childhood, or the cost of living would be truly outrageous.

At puberty, the onset of surging sex hormones is accompanied by one last spurt in growth. After this point, any further growth is only circumferential.

Bear in mind that the rate of growth is not always steady. In other words, babies often grow in spurts. If your grandchild has a limited illness or has become engrossed in one of the many developmental skills that he must conquer, his growth rate may *temporarily* decline. Also, keep in mind that bigger is not better. Obesity at any age is undesirable and should be avoided.

Rates of Growth

From birth on, three parameters of growth—height, weight, and head circumference—will be meticulously measured and recorded when your grandchild goes for checkups with the doctor. You will probably hear parents speak (and even brag) about which "percentile" their young one is growing in. For example, an average child would measure at the 50th percentile in height. This means that half the children his age are shorter and the other half are taller.

Some general rules can be applied for predicting the growth of the average-sized grandbaby. He should double his birthweight by five months, triple it by one year, and quadruple it by two years. The average increase in height is 10 to 12 inches during the first year and 5 inches during the second. Babies who were smaller at birth usually grow at a slower rate. On the other end of the scale, heftier newborns generally augment their body mass at a somewhat slower pace

Development

While your grandchild is growing, she is also busy mastering various developmental tasks. That is, she is learning about her body and how to make it work.

Developmental skills are learned in an orderly, predictable sequence. The age at which an infant actually masters a particular skill is subject to much normal variation. Every child approaches the world with his own unique style. Each has his own special talents, his own weaknesses. If your grandchild isn't walking by his first birthday (and plenty of babies aren't), look at the many other things he has accomplished.

Human development is roughly divided into four categories: gross motor, fine motor, language, and social.

Motor, Muscular, or Physical Development

The first two categories concern the infant's ability to interact physically with his environment. *Gross motor skills*, such as sitting, crawling, and walking, are governed by the big, less precise muscles. *Fine motor skills* require the coordination of the small, more exacting muscles. The acquisition of hand-eye coordination is the focus of fine motor development.

During the first three months of your grandbaby's life, reflexes rule much of his behavior. These newborn reflexes gradually fade

125

~ 6 months

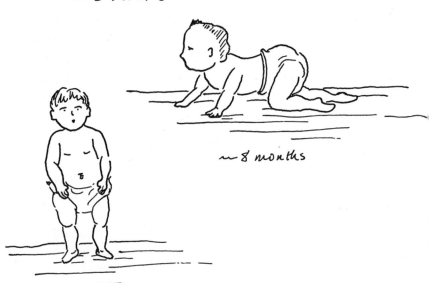

~ 8 months

~ 12 months

and, as they do, are replaced by smoother, more purposeful movements such as removing Granny's glasses from her face. Each day, your grandbaby moves more competently. So, look out! It is never too early to move dangerous and fragile objects out of Junior's reach.

Physical development follows three general patterns:

1) Muscular development progresses from head to toe. In other words, the struggle against the forces of gravity begins with learning to lift and hold the head in an upright position. Later, the torso becomes strong enough to maintain a sitting position, the hips

become vigorous enough to be lifted into a crawl stance, and lastly, the legs become steady enough to support standing.

2) The acquisition of strength and coordination of the limbs begins close to the body and moves outward. Your grandchild will first learn to coordinate her arm movements at the shoulder, then the elbows, then the wrists. Adroit manipulations of the fingers comes last.

3) An infant's physical responses to the environment are, at first, general. For example, if you dangle a red ball over your supine three-month-old grandbaby, he may smile, vigorously cycle his arms and legs, and attempt to swipe at the ball with both arms. After he is a few months older, he will smile as he expertly grabs the ball (or your glasses) with one hand.

According to one old wives's tale, you shouldn't allow an infant to bear weight on his legs or he will become bowlegged. Supporting your grandbaby while he stands for short periods of time actually increases muscular development. Your grandbaby will let you know when he is ready for this kind of activity by bouncing and shrieking with delight when you stand him up.

Language Development

In addition to holding the baby, one of the most important things that parents and grandparents can do (if they look forward to the day Junior can say heart-warming things like, "Can I borrow five bucks?") is to *talk* to him. Your verbal responsiveness promotes your grandbaby's listening skills and language recognition.

Within the first four weeks, your grandbaby should begin to make throaty sounds that are quite distinct from the other noises emanating from his mouth notably crying. During the third month of life, he may surprise you with boisterous laughter and squealing noises. By 8 to 12 weeks, your grandbaby will begin to make vowels sounds in the form of cooing noises. During the second half of the first year, he will make repetitive babbling sounds such as "dada" or "mama." As he approaches his first birthday, these vocalizations will apply specifically to those two people.

127

Beginning the second year of life, your grandbaby will slowly and gradually add new words to his vocabulary. You'll probably notice that his understanding of the spoken word far outpaces his ability to verbally express himself. Although your grandchild may feign ignorance when asked to please brush his teeth, he will immediately dash to the kitchen when you ask him, "Would you like a cookie?"

During the second half of the second year, your grandchild's progress will accelerate noticeably. He may imitate every word you utter (so, watch what you say). Your grandchild will be able to point to and name body parts. Furthermore, he will begin making small phrases by putting two or three words together to express important desires like, "More cookie, please."

You can stimulate your grandbaby's language development by chatting with her as you change, bathe, and feed her, and by naming things in her environment.

Social or Personal Development

In the realm of social development, your grandbaby will be learning important cultural skills such as smiling, interacting on a personal level with other humans, feeding, dressing, and washing herself.

The first sign of social behavior is the social smile, meaning your grandbaby smiles, not because he has gas or is having a pleasant dream, but because he sees your smiling face. Such responsive smiling begins anywhere within the first eight weeks of life. You can reinforce his efforts by smiling back.

From the time of birth, your grandbaby will actively study human faces. By three months of age, he will learn to discriminate familiar from unfamiliar faces. Sometime during the second half of the first year, your grandbaby will probably begin to react to strangers with suspicion or fear.

Stranger anxiety is accompanied by separation anxiety. A baby may become quite distraught upon being delivered by his mother into the hands of a babysitter (or even into your loving arms if he has not seen you for a while). During this phase, it helps if you keep a discreet distance at first, giving your grandchild a chance to warm up to you. If the parents leave, your grandchild probably will fuss only for a short time before

128

being distracted into play. After the second year of life, he will have a much easier time separating from his mother or father.

Feeding skills are deemed very important in our society. Around the first birthday, your grandbaby will be coordinated enough to learn to drink from a cup. Unfortunately, he will initially demonstrate more skill at picking up his cup than returning it smoothly to the table. Spills are not usually deliberate. During the next six months, he will also make great strides in learning to eat with a spoon. After the 18th month, you won't need to hose down the entire dining room after meals.

Toward the end of the second year of life, he will not only be able to remove his garments but will actually be able to dress himself. It may take him a good twenty minutes to do so, and his taste in clothes may be somewhat eccentric. Nevertheless, independence is a trait to nurture.

You can foster the development of social skills in your grandchild by offering him your uncritical, loving support. If you spend time teaching your grandchild to do things like throw a ball, pot a plant, and bake bread, you will give his self-confidence a boost. Your investment in your grandchild will help him grow up to be a secure adult.

Table of Developmental Milestones

(This list represents the age at which the *average* baby attains these skills. Skills are usually mastered at the end of the time period listed.)

1st Week
focuses at a distance of about 8 inches
can hear and localize sounds

1st Month
lifts head when placed on stomach
studies faces and objects
smiles
begins to vocalize (other than crying)

2nd Month
visually prefers faces to objects
brings hands together

3rd Month
distinguishes strange from familiar faces
switches from reflex to voluntary body
    control
holds head steady when supported in a
    sitting position
starts to grasp objects such as a rattle
crying decreases markedly
laughs

4th Month
sits with support
reaches for objects (with a swiping,
    somewhat inaccurate motion)
begins babbling

5th Month
rolls over
bears weight on legs
turns to voice

6th Month
sits without support
raking grasp (grasps using entire hand)
feeds self crackers
initially shy with strangers (this goes on
    for a few months)

7th Month
when supported under arms, stands ,
    bears weight, and bounces
grasps, manipulates, and bangs objects
enjoys playing peek-a-boo

8th Month
pulls to a stand
gets self to a sitting position
crawls (this is variable; some normal
    babies never crawl)
imitates speech sounds

9th Month
cruises (i.e., walks holding onto furniture)
pincer (thumb to finger) grasp

10th Month
stands alone briefly

11th Month
says a few intelligible words like "Mama"
    or "Dada"
climbs up stairs (on all fours)

12th Month
plays ball
drinks from a cup
stands well alone
begins to walk
indicates desires (in ways other
    than crying)

Chapter Ten

SLIPPERY WHEN WET

A Review of Infant Care for
Those Wise and Experienced

Most of the nuts and bolts of taking care of a newborn haven't changed very much over the years. But, baby-care skills do get a little rusty if you haven't used them for a few decades.

Most parents now receive some sort of education about basic baby care before they are turned loose upon their newborn. In the event that you will be involved in the care of your grandbaby, this chapter summarizes the standard spiel given to new parents.

Holding Your Grandbaby

Your newly born grandbaby's head is like a watermelon relative to the rest of her body, and the muscles in the neck are like wet noodles. Therefore, paying proper attention to supporting your grandbaby's head and neck will avoid the embarrassment of letting her head bob pathetically. You don't want the parents to think you don't know what you are doing, after all!

Not unlike their grown-up counterparts, babies dislike feeling physically insecure. (Think about the queasy feeling you get just watching James Bond free-fall out of an airplane.) After spending the past several months tightly flexed inside the womb, babies tend to respond with distress to sudden movements that leave their extended arms and legs flailing. Swaddling your grandbaby with all extremities held close to her body will make her feel secure. Snuggling her close to your body will add to your mutual contentment.

Diapering

Doubtless, you have not forgotten that babies require a long period of time to develop into civilized beings. In other words, children are not potty trained as quickly as is a golden retriever. This is an understatement. Scientific surveys reveal that it takes years to totally toilet train a human. In the interim, babies reflexedly and unabashedly empty both bladder and bowel. Because elimination ranks right up there with sucking as one of the few skills your grandbaby has mastered, he delights in demonstrating his prowess.

A long time ago, our practical ancestors invented the diaper or nappy, an ingenious device designed to catch human excrement before it lands on Granddad's lap. Modern technology

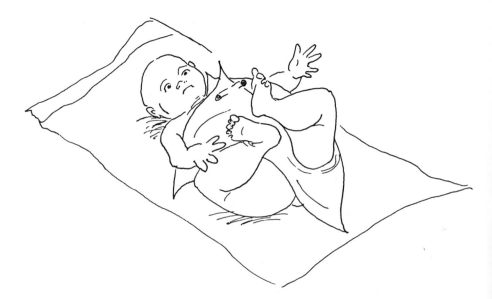

now provides caretakers of infants with two basic types of diapers: the cloth diaper and the disposable diaper.

You have probably had vast personal experience with cotton diapers. You fold (now you can purchase them prefolded) the diaper, wrap it artistically around baby's bottom, fasten it with pins, and cover it with a waterproof pant. A technological advance since your diapering days is the discovery of Velcro and its adaptation to hold together both diapers and diaper covers.

Disposable diapers consist of layers of various synthetic materials. They are also wrapped around the baby's bottom, but are held in place by adhesive tabs. As opposed to cloth diapers, which are meant to be laundered after each use, the manufacturers recommend that you discard disposable diapers when soiled.

Comparison of Cloth and Disposable Diapers

	Cloth	Disposable
Advantages	less expensive, recyclable, often better for baby's skin (fewer rashes)	slighter faster to change, more convenient (especially when traveling), very absorbent
Disadvantages	someone must wash them (better someone else than you, e.g., a diaper service), are usually changed more frequently	more expensive, not recyclable nor readily biodegradable*, may contribute to diaper rash, untreated waste ends up in our sanitary land fills

* A new disposable diaper that claims to be 99.4% biodegradable is on the market.

133

Genital Hygiene

You (as opposed to the average teen-aged baby-sitter) know that diapers should be changed as soon after elimination as possible. The goal is to avoid prolonged contact of irritating substances with delicate baby skin. A damp cloth, cotton ball, or disposable premoistened towelette can be used to clean the skin at diaper changes.

Creams and ointments can be applied to the diaper area. Baby powders, cornstarch, and talc are not only without benefit, but can actually harm your grandbaby if she inhales these particles (especially talc) into her lungs.

Baby granddaughters should always be wiped from front to back to avoid contaminating the urethra and vagina with bowel organisms, because they can lead to bladder infections. Clean between all the skin folds.

Infant grandsons should also be cleaned from front to back. If you grandson is uncircumcised, *gently* retract the foreskin as far as it will easily slide and clean the penis with warm water.

If your grandson has been recently circumcised, extra care is necessary to prevent wound infection and subsequent scarring.

A word of caution: As you know, one way boys differ from girls is that they possess a penis capable of propelling a powerful jet of urine long distances. Baby boys seem to take great pride at demonstrating their aim, especially when an adoring grandparent is bent over fumbling with the diaper.

Diaper Rashes

If your grandbaby develops a diaper rash, her skin may have been irritated by urine and feces, chemicals in the disposable diapers, or residual laundry detergent on cloth diapers. Such a rash is treated by avoidance of the irritant—changing the diapers more frequently, switching to a different type of diaper, using a milder detergent, and rinsing the diapers more thoroughly. After cleaning and drying the diaper area, an ointment (Vaseline, Desitin, A & D) can be applied to protect the skin from irritants.

More serious diaper rashes can be caused by infections with yeast or bacteria. The correct diagnosis is necessary to initiate the appropriate antibiotic treatment. If a diaper rash does not start to clear up in a couple of days or looks particularly bad, your grandbaby should see a physician.

Cord Care

The umbilical cord stump should be cleaned (usually with alcohol-soaked cotton swabs) three to four times a day. A small amount of crusty discharge is normal. Bleeding, foul smelling drainage, redness, and swelling are abnormal and should be reported to a doctor. The cord will fall off between one and three weeks.

Nails

A baby's fingernails are nearly as sharp as a kitten's. However, most kittens do not scratch themselves, preferring to claw the upholstery instead. Your grandbaby's nails should be kept short to protect herself. Wait to cut the nails until they are free from the underlying skin. Then use small scissors, nail clippers, or a nail file.

Nose

See Chapter nine.

Ears

As the saying goes, "Never try to put anything smaller than your elbow in your ear." No one should attempt to clean the inside of a baby's ear canal with Q-tips or the like. This tends to push dirt and wax deeper and can hurt the baby. Ear wax is normal and has a protective function. Gently wipe ear debris away as it emerges at the entrance of the ear canal using a Q-tip or a cotton swab.

Bathing Grandbaby

Your newborn grandchild does not need a bath every day. A bath every two to three days is sufficient. Newborns often find bath time disagreeable because of the inherent insecurity of being naked with arms and legs flailing. Later, bath time is usually a fun time—provided parents and grandparents have made it so. There are two main types of baths: sponge baths and tub baths. In the first weeks before the cords falls off and a circumcised penis has healed, you or the parents should sponge-bathe the baby. (Usually, spot cleaning at head and tail suffices.)

After that time, you may tub-bathe your grandbaby. Bear in mind that, from your grandbaby's perspective, the bathtub is a cavernous, slippery place. An infant bathtub or a clean, plastic dishpan allows you and your grandbaby to feel more in control.

Never leave your grandbaby unattended during bath time. Infants and small children can slip and drown in only a few inches of water.

Bathing Tips

Be sure you have everything you will need ready and within grasp before you begin:

☐   a warm room

☐   a grandbaby who is in a pleasant mood

☐   a clean washcloth and cotton balls (for cleaning the eyes and the circumcision site)

☐   a basin of warm water for sponge-bathing or a tub of warm water

☐   mild soap, mild ("no tears") shampoo

☐   a dry bath towel

☐   clean diaper, pins, diaper cover, and clean clothes

☐   a raincoat to protect yourself from grandbaby's exuberant splashing

---

Dressing Grandbaby

For the first couple of months after birth, an infant is ineffi-
cient at conserving body heat. Therefore, babies need to be kept
warm. Unless the house is unusually cold, a diaper, T-shirt,
sleeper, and surrounding shawl or blanket are sufficient indoor
attire for your grandbaby.

How do you know whether your grandbaby is adequately
dressed? If he is chilled, your grandbaby will indicate his discomfort by being unusually still or by crying. His hands and feet
may feel cool. In this case, do the obvious things: bring him into
a warm room, wrap him in blankets, cuddle him, and provide a
warm feeding.

On the other extreme, if your grandbaby is overdressed, he
will feel warm and sweaty and appear flushed and fussy. Of
course, you would want to remedy the situation by removing
some clothing. If he is very warm, you can sponge him with
tepid (not cold) water and fan him dry. In the event that your
grandbaby is not overdressed, yet feels warm to your touch,
check his temperature with a thermometer (see Chapter thirteen
for how to take your grandbaby's temperature).

Provided your grandbaby is appropriately dressed, you
needn't worry about drafts. Drafts alone do not cause illness.

Dealing with a Crying Grandbaby

One million dollars says that not one of you grandparents has forgotten that babies cry. Babies have a limited repertoire of communication skills. Nonetheless, your grandbaby will quickly learn that crying loudly is an effective means of attracting attention. If your grandbaby happens to be the kind of baby who seems to cry a lot, assure the parents that they are not to blame.

Some of the Reasons That Babies Cry:

☐ hunger

☐ need to suck (a need distinct from hunger)

☐ wet/soiled diaper (although many babies seem to be totally content to sit in wet, poopy diapers)

☐ fear (of strangers, being separated from loved ones, loud noises, purple monsters)

☐ overstimulation (e.g., you have been alternately tossing baby in the air and singing "Itsy, Bitsy Spider" for two hours)

☐ understimulation (i.e., boredom)

☐ expression of anger or frustration

☐ pain/discomfort (too warm, too cold, left in uncomfortable position, colic*, teething, illness)

☐ exercise (try it: a great toner for the muscles of the face and abdomen)

* In case you hav e never witnessed a baby with colic... It occurs in about 10 percent of babies. It is not a disease. It is marked by unexplained bouts of crying that often occur in the evening and can last up to three hours in an otherwise happy, healthy, well-fed infant between two weeks and three months of age. During an episode of colic, the baby draws up his legs, tenses his abdomen, and turns red in the face. Pediatricians still don't know the cause of colic, nor do they have a cure. Colic is *not* due to excessive intestinal gas, bad parenting, or imperfect grandparenting.

Some Things You Can Do
to End the Crying Binge

☐ wrap snugly, hold, cuddle, massage

☐ feed your grandbaby or give her a pacifier if she isn't hungry but needs to suck

☐ rock, walk with your grandbaby in your arms or in a front carrier, infant swing

☐ talk or sing to baby, play soft music on a radio, phonograph, or music box

☐ change the diaper

☐ remove or add clothing as indicated

☐ give your grandbaby a warm bath

☐ try to distract your grandbaby (dance and sing to selections from "South Pacific")

☐ Repeat these maneuvers. Eventually, you will exhaust your grandbaby who will, in desperation, fall asleep. Alternatively, *you* can give up and go to sleep.

Note: Seriously, if your grandbaby is inconsolable, is less than two months old *and* acts ill, has been crying for more than three hours, has a high-pitched cry, seems to be in pain, call a physician. (See Chapter thirteen for a list of signs of illness.)

Most Important Appliances in the Care and Feeding of Grandbaby

Chapter Eleven

FEEDING GRANDBABY

What Goes in Often Ends Up on
Your Cashmere Sweater

What should babies eat? Most people, even those inexperienced with infants, know that babies consume large volumes of milk.

At the turn of the century, babies were kept on a diet consisting of milk until the first birthday. As time passed, parents introduced supplemental foods to their infants progressively earlier. Eventually, parents attempted to stuff pabulum into their babies' tiny mouths not long after they emerged from the womb.

Currently, most pediatricians feel that for the first four to six months of life, babies need nothing more than milk to satisfy their nutritional needs. Why do they recommend this delay?

1) Before four months of age, babies are endowed with a very powerful tongue thrusting reflex, which causes any solids placed in their small oral cavities to be propelled right back out and onto the feeder's dry-clean-only garment.

2) Babies lack the intestinal maturity to properly digest foods other than human milk and reasonable facsimiles thereof. If you feed junior spinach, he will reward you for your efforts with a green poop.

141

3) Premature introduction of various foods may lead to the future development of allergies. Also, these foods may cause immediate allergic reactions with associated hives, vomiting, diarrhea, weight loss, anemia, and asthma.

4) Small infants lack the motor skills necessary to avert their heads, push the spoon away, or otherwise indicate satiety in a socially appropriate manner.

5) Worse yet, these babies may become obese. Some individuals find roly-poly babies cute. The big concern is that fat babies might remain overweight. Few individuals consider 300-pound adults cute.

So, what kind of milk should a baby drink? Modern babies have two main options. They can either feast upon human breast milk or infant formula. Which is preferable?

Formula manufacturers will freely disclose that most infant formulas are based upon cow's milk, which was originally designed for baby cows. Baby humans come equipped with digestive systems unlike that of baby cows. It turns out that human breast milk is much better suited for baby humans than is cow's milk. These astonishing findings have led many authorities to state firmly, "Breast is best." Actually, each method has its advantages and disadvantages for the mother-baby duo.

Breast-Feeding

You may well recall that during the 1950s, women were not given much encouragement to breast-feed their babies. During that decade, fewer than 25 percent of mothers nursed their babies. Most who were brave enough to try quit by the end of the first month. Why, when prior to this time nearly all babies were breast-fed—in fact, had to be breast-fed to survive?

By this time in the history of processed foods, special infant formulas had been developed that were strongly promoted by their manufacturers, as well as by doctors and nurses. Doctors often told new mothers that they would not be capable of producing sufficient milk. Rigid hospital nursery schedules and staff unsupportive of breast-feeding created a climate unconducive to nursing an infant.

142

After receiving a deluge of advice to the contrary and numerous fliers and free samples from formula sales representatives, an occasional courageous woman persevered and nursed her baby. Not uncommonly, her physician would urge her at least to supplement her breast-feeding with a few bottles of infant formula "to be sure the baby was getting enough to eat."

Unfortunately, these formula supplements were often the kiss of death for successful nursing. The more bottles a baby receives, the less the baby suckles at the breast and, therefore, the less milk the breast makes. Breasts are strong supporters of the supply and demand theory of production. Given enough breast stimulation, most women can successfully nurse their babies.

Many women became sufficiently discouraged or disinterested and never tried to nurse their babies. Before hospital discharge, doctors routinely prescribed pills or injections to dry up their milk and ordered their breasts tightly bound to decrease some of the discomfort.

In the late '60s and early '70s, breast-feeding again became popular. This resurgence was, in part, linked to the natural childbirth movement with its emphasis on following the dictates of instinct and physiology. Probably equally important was scientific data that revealed that breast-feeding is in many ways superior to formula feeding. And, because fashions shift like a pendulum, breast-feeding was attractive to some women simply because it was something their mothers did not do. The way your grandchild is fed will probably mirror the way your mother fed you.

Pros and Cons of Breast-Feeding

Pros

☐ Mother's milk contains antibodies and other substances that help defend a baby against infection.

☐ Breast milk is germ free. No sterilization or refrigeration is necessary (unless milk is expressed and stored for future use).

☐ Breast milk is "free," unless you consider that the lactating woman eats voraciously to make up the extra 500 kilo-calories a day she expends (and someone has to pay the grocery bill).

☐ Breast-feeding helps the mother lose extra weight gained during the pregnancy because of the calories required to produce milk.

☐ Breast-feeding satisfies a baby's need to suck more effectively than does bottle-feeding.

☐ The more an infant suckles, the more breast milk is produced. Also, the content of breast milk varies to meet a baby's differing nutritional needs.

☐ Breast-fed babies are less likely to become obese.

☐ Mother's milk is easier to digest.

☐ Breast-fed babies are less likely to develop allergies.

☐ Nursing is usually a physically and emotionally satisfying experience for baby and mother.

☐ Early nursing stimulates the release of a hormone from the mother's brain that causes her milk to "let down." This hormone (oxytocin) also stimulates the uterus to contract to its original size, thus speeding recovery and helping to prevent postpartum hemorrhage.

☐ Regular nursing inhibits ovulation (but is not a very reliable form of birth control).

Cons

☐ Breast-feeding requires the mother's presence, which causes some women to feel tied down. A nursing mother can prepare "relief bottles" of either expressed breast milk or formula when she needs a respite.

☐ Modesty. Some women feel shy and awkward about nursing. Other mothers are at ease discretely nursing their babies in the most public of places.

☐ Diet. Nursing women must continue to pay attention to their diet due to the increased nutritional demands. Furthermore, alcohol, caffeine, nicotine, and other drugs and environmental contaminants in food and water can cross into breast milk and adversely affect the baby.

☐ Rest. Because nursing does require energy, a woman needs to make sure she gets enough rest.

Helpful Hints for Grandparents of Nursing Babies

■ Resist the temptation to ask repeatedly, "Are you sure he's getting enough to eat?" If you were told to supplement your nursing baby's diet with formula feedings, you may find yourself clinging to the belief that the average female breast is incapable of producing a sufficient volume of milk. If your grandbaby wets at least six diapers a day and is steadily gaining weight, she is getting enough milk. Also, remember that babies cry for reasons other than hunger.

■ Keep in mind that larger breasts have more fat cells, not more milk glands. A less bosomy woman should be able to make plenty of milk for her baby.

■ Be supportive of the mother's desire to breast-feed, even if you feel it went out of fashion with outhouses. Self-confidence is essential to successful breast-feeding.

■ If you find yourself feeling annoyed because your daughter is nursing your grandbaby, ask yourself whether you might feel jealous. If you are a grandmother whose own attempt to nurse was thwarted, you may even feel anger at being deprived. It is not uncommon for fathers and grandparents to feel left out of this special and intimate relationship with the baby. Remind yourself that you can nurture your grandchild in many other ways.

■ Avoid remarking with indignant surprise, "You're *still* nursing that child!!?" In some cultures, it is not at all unusual for women to nurse their children for three or four years. In the United States more women are nursing their babies for more than a year. However, many of these women are so sensitive to the incredulous expressions of their friends and relatives that they breast-feed surreptitiously. Weaning is a private decision between mother and child.

Bottle-Feeding

Although breast milk is the ideal food source for infants, nursing a baby may be neither desirable nor feasible. A mother may not wish to breast-feed for a variety of reasons: she is chronically ill or fatigued; she is the kind of person who only disrobes completely to bathe; she holds a job in New York while baby is cared for by domestics in California; her husband resents the idea of anyone else having intimate access to her breasts. Or, she may be one of the very few women not capable of producing sufficient breast milk.

Pros and Cons of Bottle-Feeding

Pros

☐ Allows more people to participate in feeding baby (even in the middle of the night).

☐ Frees the mother if she requires time away from her baby.

☐ Fewer physical demands on the mother.

Cons

☐ More expensive.

☐ Less convenient from the standpoint that the formula must be purchased, stored, and prepared (this convenience factor seems exaggerated in the middle of the night).

☐ Because the infant receives no immunities in formula and because formula can become contaminated with microorganisms, the risk of infection is increased.

☐ Increased risk of developing allergies.

☐ Increased tendency to infant obesity.

147

Sometimes, the other member of the mother-infant duo creates the stumbling block to breast-feeding. For example, a baby may be unable to suckle effectively because of illness or a structural abnormality of the mouth. Even under such adverse circumstances, a mother can express her milk if her infant receives tube feedings. This way, her baby still receives many of the benefits of breast milk.

Regardless of the reasons, if your daughter elects to bottle-feed your grandbaby, she should not be made to feel guilty. Modern formulas are designed to simulate breast milk as closely as possible and quite adequately meet the average infant's nutritional needs. If your grandbaby is cuddled during bottle-feedings, he derives physical and emotional fulfillment similar to a breast-fed baby.

Types of Formulas and Bottle Preparation

Formulas can be purchased in ready-to-use form, concentrate, or powder. The latter two require the addition of water. In some cities where the water has been adequately treated, plain tap water can be used. In many other locales, the water must first be boiled. The water can either be boiled before addition to the bottle, or the formula-filled bottle can be placed in a pot of boiling water for sterilization.

You may have given your babies formula made by mixing evaporated milk with boiled water and sugar or corn syrup. Parents can still give their babies evaporated milk formula. However, bottle sterilization and vitamin supplementation are required. The cost is about the same as using a commercial formula. Not surprisingly, most parents now use commercial formulas.

Different formulas vary in their composition. Unless babies have an illness or an allergy to cow's milk, most drink cow's milk-based formulas. Alternatives (for infants who cannot digest cow's milk) include a soy formula or a predigested milk. Some doctors recommend a soy formula for breast-fed babies (who receive an occasional formula bottle) to minimize the risk of development of allergies.

Many parents and grandparents wonder whether infants need supplemental fluids other than breast milk or formula (particularly water or sugar water during warm weather). Usually not. Breast milk and formula are composed largely of water. Supplemental water bottles only deprive baby of the calories and nutrients present in milk. Under most circumstances, a baby with an increased fluid requirement should simply drink more breast milk or formula.

At times it is appropriate or even preferable for a baby to drink fluids other than mother's milk or formula. For example, clear liquids may be recommended by a doctor if the infant has had vomiting or diarrhea. Also, after solid foods are introduced (between the fourth and sixth month), your grandbaby can drink diluted fruit juices.

Your grandbaby shouldn't drink regular cow's milk until the end of her first year (at which time the doctor will recommend the switch). Until then, your grandbaby's intestinal tract and kidneys are not sufficiently mature to handle the much higher protein and salt content of cow's milk.

You may be surprised to learn that it is no longer considered essential to warm the milk before giving it to your grandbaby. She can take her bottle straight from the refrigerator. Gone are the days of listening to a screaming hungry infant while bringing the milk to a balmy temperature.

One proviso is that a regularly breast-fed infant who is accustomed to body temperature fluids may appreciate a warmed supplemental bottle. You can take the chill off refrigerated milk by running the bottle under warm tap water. Heating formula in the microwave is not recommended because of the dangers of overheating the milk and of breaking the bottle.

Because the normal bacteria living inside your grandbaby's mouth contaminate and quickly multiply within bottled milk, you should discard any remaining milk after a feeding. Also, discard any bottles of milk that have been sitting around at room temperature for several hours regardless of whether baby has consumed any or not. (If such waste makes you think of the world's hungry children, send a check to an organization struggling to combat famine, but throw away that milk.)

Refrigerate prepared bottles until it's time to use them. Unused formula bottles should be discarded after 24 hours. Open formula cans should be thrown out after 48 hours. Because of the antibacterial agents found in breast milk, expressed milk can be safely stored in the refrigerator at least five days. Expressed breast milk can be stored in the freezer for about two weeks or in the deep freeze for two months.

How and When to Bottle-Feed Babies—Some Changes

You may have been told that it was important to keep your baby on a rigid feeding schedule. More recently, the notion of *demand feeding* of both breast- and bottle-fed infants has gained wider acceptance. Quite simply, the baby is fed whenever and for as long as he seems hungry. Newborns usually want to eat at frequent, and sometimes irregular, intervals. After about three months of age, most babies have worked themselves into a rhythm of eating every three or four hours.

Bottle propping is now discouraged. One reason is that it robs a baby of his need for physical contact. Babies deprived of tender loving care do not grow and develop at a normal rate and cannot be expected to snag jobs as wealthy corporate lawyers who will finance their grandparents' retirement to Bermuda.

Another problem with supping supine with a propped bottle is the increased risk of ear infections due to milk dripping into the middle ear. Also, the baby may drift off into slumber with a mouthful of milk or juice, which coats the teeth with sugar and thus promotes tooth decay. The older babe who can hold his own bottle should not be allowed to take a bottle to bed for these same reasons.

In another philosophical shift, most pediatricians have stopped recommending that parents add *cereal* to milk bottles. In the past, weary parents, desperately seeking a good night's sleep, frequently supplemented the formula with cereal in hopes of satisfying baby's hunger more efficiently.

Adding cereal to the bottle is undesirable for several reasons. Milk contains more calories per ounce than most solids can provide. Furthermore, young babies can't digest cereal very well and may develop allergies if introduced to it too soon. In order to force the cereal through the nipple, the hole must be enlarged. Thus, when the baby sucks, she is gulping down more food. But because the baby is seeking to satisfy her need to suck, she will drink from the bottle past the point of satiating her hunger. The potential result is obesity. Finally, a recent study found no difference between the sleep patterns of infants given cereal supplements and those given unadulterated formula.

150

1950's baby - scheduled feeding

1980's baby
Demand Feeding.

When to Begin Solid Foods

As mentioned at the beginning of this chapter, pediatricians now recommend that solid foods not be introduced until an infant is between four and six months of age, when he can actually swallow and digest a few food items other than milk. Another prerequisite to feeding your grandbaby solids is that you acquire a rain slicker, a full-length bib for Junior, a tiled feeding cubicle complete with hose, a spoon with a ten-foot-long handle, and a washer and drier.

Which Foods First

The rule here is to only introduce one new food at a time. If your grandbaby tolerates that food well for a week, another type of food can be introduced. Otherwise, if your grandbaby samples several new foods at once and has a bad reaction, no one will know which food did not agree with him.

Cereals

Cereals (especially rice cereal) are good first foods. Many precooked cereals are specially prepared for infants and are usually fortified with iron. Because wheat has a tendency to cause allergic reactions, babies shouldn't eat wheat cereal (and other wheat products in quantity) for several months.

Fruits

Most babies love fruits because of their sweetness. Mashed or strained fruits, such as ripe bananas, stewed apples, peaches, pears, prunes, and apricots, are good first foods. Citrus fruits, pineapple, and strawberries are commonly allergenic and should be delayed until the end of the first year.

Juices

Even at six months of age, your grandbaby should still be breast-fed four times a day or receive 24 to 28 ounces of formula a day. Juices, therefore, should not replace milk feedings.

> **Signs of food intolerance:** vomiting, diarrhea, gassiness, skin rash (hives), weight loss, anemia.

Clear juices should be diluted 2:1 with water. Dark juices should be diluted 5:1 with water.

Vegetables

Two to four weeks after your grandbaby has demonstrated that he can tolerate fruits and cereals, he can try vegetables. It is best to begin with the yellow vegetables.

Milk Products

In the absence of an allergy to cow's milk, yogurt, cottage cheese, other cheeses, and low-fat milk can be added to your grandbaby's diet at the end of his first year.

Eggs

Eggs are usually delayed until nine months of age. Egg whites head the list of foods likely to cause allergy and should be introduced cautiously. Because of the high cholesterol content of the egg yolk, your grandchild shouldn't eat eggs more than three to four times a week.

Meats

After your grandbaby is tolerating cereal, fruit and vegetables, he can try meats, starting with finely ground white meats (chicken, turkey, and fish, excluding shellfish). Legumes are a good alternative to meat as a protein source.

Nuts

Peanut butter can be started at nine months. Whole peanuts and other nuts are dangerous for babies and toddlers because they can be inhaled into the airways.

Food Consistency

At first foods should be strained, finely ground, or pureed. Around six to seven months, babies become interested in feeding themselves (you, the cat, the carpet) "finger foods" such as pieces of cooked carrots, cooked beans, bananas, cheese, fish, dried bread strips, and biscuits. By nine months, foods should be mashed instead of strained. Toward the end of the first year, foods should be left lumpy or chopped into small pieces.

Foods That Can Be Dangerous

The following foods are hazardous for infants and toddlers because they are easily choked upon: nuts, whole corn kernels, popcorn, potato and corn chips, hot dogs, certain dry cereals, hard candies, raw peas, whole and unseeded grapes, and berries.

Honey should not be given to infants because of the risk of contamination from the botulism bacteria.

Processed versus Fresh, Home Prepared Foods

The manufacturers of baby foods have come a long way in eliminating or reducing undesirable substances such as salt, monosodium glutamate, sugar, fillers, artificial flavorings, food coloring, and harmful preservatives from their products. Also, many processed baby foods are vitamin fortified. Yet, many parents and grandparents prefer to prepare fresh foods for their children. Little additional time is required to do so. Good books discussing baby food preparation abound.

Vegetarian Families

Should you worry if your adult children and grandchildren follow a vegetarian diet? Not necessarily. Some vegetarians limit themselves to a strict diet, excluding all animal products including milk and eggs. Such a limited diet is not appropriate for a small child. Vegetarians (including children) who include milk, eggs, and occasional seafood or poultry are not likely to suffer from nutritional deficiencies.

Anyone who maintains a vegetarian diet should know how to combine various food groups to satisfy nutritional needs. Infants and children can thrive on a proper vegetarian diet. The problem (particularly with a strict vegetarian regime) is that the typical child with a small, finicky appetite may not eat enough of each essential food group to ensure optimal nutrition. The success of a vegetarian diet in a small child is, therefore, variable.

Eating Habits

The consumption of food by an infant or toddler is no trivial matter in the eyes of most parents and grandparents. If a child is

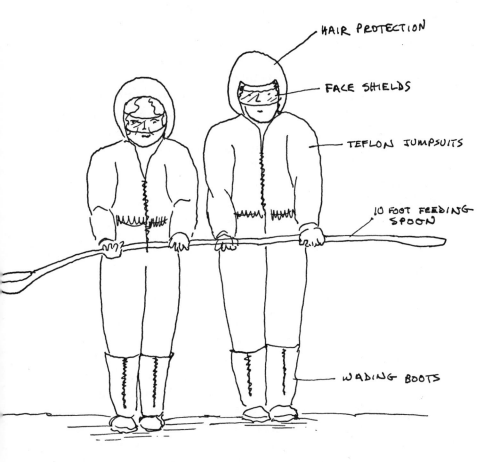

Protective Feeding Gear for Grandparents

perceived as eating too little or too much, all kinds of parental and grandparental anxieties can result.

Generally, children eat to appetite. They eat when they are hungry and quit when they are satiated. It is often the adults who pervert nature's "appestat." If a child is growing normally, he is probably eating the right amount of food.

Adults who hover over a child, trying to encourage, or worse, coerce him into eating more, will communicate to him that a problem exists. Then, eating may become a real problem. Tense adults at mealtime make for a tense child who loses his appetite or learns to use eating as a means to control the adults. Better to offer nutritious food in a pleasant environment and remove the remainder when it is clear that Junior has finished (e.g., when Junior starts to create pop art with the leftovers).

Another aspect of eating that can be viewed as problematic is the mess that normally accompanies mealtime. Masterful hand-eye coordination takes much time and experience. Babies are not born knowing how to maneuver spoons to their mouths. That skill comes with time and practice. When your grandbaby demonstrates readiness to self-feed, don't discourage this independent gesture.

Throwing food off the high-chair is another feeding behavior that can be distressing to adults. About the ninth month, infants learn to pick up and purposefully release an object. The release part is harder to master (which is why a baby usually spills the cup of juice when trying to set it down rather than when picking it up). Repeatedly dropping an object from the high-chair and watching the downward trajectory can become a favorite pastime. Toward the end of the first year, dropping objects gives way to deliberately throwing them.

About this time, parents and grandparents may cease to recognize the educational value of such diversions and communicate to Junior that throwing a tennis ball is permissible whereas throwing handfuls of mashed potato is not. One way to try to eliminate food slinging is to say no, calmly the first time, louder the next time. Often, such admonitions have little effect on Junior. In this case, you may need to teach your grandbaby that this behavior is not acceptable by calmly removing him from the table each time he begins to work on his pitching arm during meals.

Remember that you are an important role model for baby. You can encourage good eating habits by setting a good example yourself. Now is the time to give up those enjoyable rituals such as spitting watermelon seeds at your spouse and eating ice cream for the main course. Otherwise, your grandchildren may point out these inconsistencies when you correct their table manners and eating habits.

Summary Rules of Thumb for Feeding Grandbaby

☐ Regardless of whether your daughter decides to breast- or bottle-feed your grandbaby, support her decision.

☐ Very few women do not have sufficient breast milk for their babies. If you encourage supplemental formula bottles, the mother's breasts will produce less milk.

☐ If your grandbaby is not breast-fed, he should receive a special infant formula and not cow's milk for the better part of the first year.

☐ All that babies require for the first four to six months of life is breast milk or formula. Generally, solid foods are not recommended before that time.

☐ Use an appropriate sterile technique when preparing and storing bottles.

☐ Discard the remainder of milk in the bottle after your grandbaby has finished eating.

☐ Hold baby and bottle; do not prop the bottle.

☐ Do not add cereal to the formula unless advised by the doctor.

☐ Introduce only one new food at a time.

☐ Never force your grandchild to eat.

☐ Encourage independence if your grandbaby is trying to feed himself—even if this entails a bit of a mess.

Chapter Twelve

CHILD REARING

Has This Changed, Too?

Although babies don't change, theories about the proper way to raise them do. Why should you even bother to learn about current child-rearing dogma now that your children are grown? Technically, you no longer bear the sole responsibility for trying to mold a little bundle of reflexes into a clean, tidy person continent of bowel and bladder who eats with a knife and fork, says "please" and "thank you," and refrains from spitting, kicking, biting, and hitting other sentient creatures.

Nevertheless, you will probably be spending time with your grandchildren and their parents. If you have an understanding of what the latest child development gurus have to say, then you are more likely to understand the parents' belief systems and are less likely to leap into futile arguments.

This is not to say that your adult children will diverge widely from the way you so skillfully raised them. Particularly if yours was a happy household, your children are quite likely to adopt a similar parenting style.

With due respect for the fact that you grandparents have had plenty of experience raising children, the remainder of this chapter provides you with brief discussions of the more dramatic shifts in child behavior philosophies.

Spoiling

Not long ago, many authorities and even some parents believed that babies were manipulative little creatures who would do anything for attention, in particular cry at all sorts of inconvenient times. Pediatricians often advised parents not to pick up their infant other than for perfunctory diaper changes and otherwise to leave the baby in her crib and "let her cry." You may have been discouraged from cuddling your baby as desired for fear of spoiling her.

For people who lack a sadistic streak, listening to a baby cry is distressing. Instinct makes us want to rush in and comfort a miserable infant. Nature probably intended for adults to react in this fashion. Responding promptly (and with love) to a baby's needs fosters the development of a happy, secure child and, in turn, a well-adjusted adult.

After years of careful observation, researchers now maintain that infants do not possess the intellectual sophistication prerequisite to the manipulation of other humans. Babies are simple creatures. They feel a need and then quickly express their desire. An infant's usual method of self-expression involves various combinations of crying, whimpering, howling, and screaming. Parents and grandparents are left with the responsibility of interpreting what the baby wants (which can seem as difficult as deciphering the Rosetta Stone).

In a philosophical reversal of sorts, modern pediatricians now encourage parents to hold and talk to their infant as much as is reasonably possible. Intimate interactions between a newborn and the other family members not only fails to spoil the baby, but actually accelerates her development.

At what age can your indulgence of your grandbaby's every need cause her to become spoiled? No one seems to know exactly at what age infants become savvy enough to develop bad habits. Most experts agree that you can't spoil a baby under three months of age. Some stretch the age limit to six or even nine months.

What constitutes a spoiled person? A spoiled person is difficult to love and does things that the rest of humanity considers unacceptable. A spoiled child makes unfair or excessive demands (usually in a whining or imperious voice), is

tyrannical, cannot endure waiting for anything, and wants to be constantly entertained.

How does one spoil a child? The older baby or child can become a bit spoiled by parents and grandparents who are over-ly eager to please, who give in to unreasonable demands or whining, who don't follow through with their own guidelines for acceptable behavior. For example, if you play with your grandchild her every waking moment, she will forget how to amuse herself. After you depart, the parents will be left to deal with a demanding, fretful little person who fancies that everyone else was put on earth to amuse Her Highness.

If you shower your grandchild with gifts, will you spoil her? Not necessarily. What matters is *not* the absolute number of gifts she receives, but *how* these gifts are given.

If your grandchild is able to manipulate you into changing your mind against your better judgment, causing you to repeatedly give in to her selfish whims, you are teaching her to be self-indulgent. If, on the other hand, you comply when your grandchild's wishes are reasonable, you are teaching her about mutual respect. The key is to set realistic limits for a child and then stick by them.

Discipline Versus Punishment

How does a parent or grandparent shape a child into a responsible, caring, sensitive adult who has learned to control natural impulses such as throwing food at siblings, drawing on the walls, and urinating on the carpet?

It has long been recognized that love is the key ingredient in turning a child into a well-adjusted adult. Most criminals suffer during childhood not from lack of discipline, but from lack of love and affection.

Most children grow up to be agreeable people because they love the important adults in their world and want to imitate them. You can do a lot to positively influence your grandchild's behavior by being a gentle, loving person worthy of emulation.

No doubt your children misbehaved on occasion despite your own impeccable deportment. This admittance implies that child rearing entails something other than good example. That something involves rewarding good behavior and discouraging unacceptable behavior.

Many parents and grandparents take for granted children's commendable conduct. Yet, all people thrive on praise. You may need to remind yourself to thank your grandchild for playing

161

quietly while you talk on the telephone, for sharing her toys with her brother, for making it through the grocery store without begging for candy, et cetera. Positive feedback increases self-esteem and usually makes the recipient want to continue to do well or even do better.

Of course, children are not angels. Very small children have poorly developed consciences. They are egocentric and often don't know when their actions are potentially harmful or dangerous. Therefore, children are bound to do things that mature adults find disagreeable or alarming. Children require guidance, consistent limits, and discipline when they overstep their bounds.

What does the term discipline mean and how does it different from punishment? *Punishment* usually gets the message across that the child did something wrong by penalizing him in some way, but fails to teach the child how to do better. *Discipline* implies that education accompanies the corrective measure.

The primary purpose of discipline is to keep children from harming themselves, other living creatures, and valued inanimate objects like your crystal. You keep children from doing wrong by pointing out the undesirable action, discouraging the repetition of that action, and by teaching them acceptable alternatives.

How did you handle your children's misbehavior? Imagine your son sitting at the dinner table throwing peas at his younger sister. Perhaps you would calmly say, "Johnny, we don't throw food at the table." Then, a little louder, "Johnny, stop throwing peas at Suzie." Then, you shriek, "STOP THAT AT ONCE OR I'LL KNOCK YOU INTO NEXT WEEK." Then, THWOK, you bean him with your dinner roll and send him snivelling to his room to fast. If that scenario sounds representative, your response mirrors that of most American parents.

Although physical punishment, yelling, and threatening *may* curtail a child's misbehavior, the moratorium is often temporary, usually lasting only as long as the authority figure is at large. Furthermore, these tactics are not without harmful side effects. Each time a child is unkindly rebuked or hit (spanked), his self-esteem erodes a bit. Additionally, the child usually responds with ugly emotions such as anger, resentment, and a desire for vengeance. (The authority figure often experiences negative feelings as well—anger, guilt, and embarrassment at losing control.) Besieged by emotional turmoil, the child quickly forgets the behavior that warranted the punishment. In fact, the child has learned little about how to be a better person.

What the child does learn is that, although he is discouraged from hitting or yelling, adults can hit and yell with impunity. Therefore, it must be all right for the biggest person to hit and yell at those smaller in stature; it must be acceptable to solve problems by being overtly aggressive. Some sociologists go so far as to blame excessive physical punishment during childhood as a cause of much of the violence in our society.

If spanking, yelling, nagging, and threatening are out, what measures can a parent or grandparent take to effectively discipline an errant child? The answer to this question depends on the age of the child and the particular misbehavior.

Discipline is inappropriate for babies under four months because they do not wittingly misbehave. For older babies, you can try one or a combination of several techniques. First of all, structure the environment when possible so that tantalizing "no-no's" are out of reach. Use distraction to derail your grandbaby from mischief (give him a rattle to substitute for your spectacles). Voice mild disapproval. Physically remove him (gently) from the undesirable activity. If the misbehavior is attention seeking (and unharmful), ignore it.

For toddlers, you can add *time-out* to your repertoire. Whether you realize it or not, you probably utilized the principle behind time-out—mild social deprivation—on your own children.

The procedure for using time-out is as follows:

1) You catch your grandson, Johnny, doing something unacceptable, such as biting your leg.

2) Calmly, you briefly state the problem: "Johnny, we don't bite people in this family. Biting hurts people."

3) Before you burst into a rage, you calmly put Johnny in a designated time-out spot. It might be a chair (or empty playpen for a toddler) in the middle of the household where he sees what is going on but cannot participate. The location is at best dull but not scary.

4) After Johnny is quietly settled in his time-out spot, he must remain there for a set period of time (approximately one minute for each year of age up to five minutes).

5) After the time is up (both you and your grandchild have had a chance to collect your wits), you go to him and quietly and briefly discuss what happened. You reaffirm that you know (hope, pray...) that he is really a good boy, that he did a naughty thing, that you will help him by putting him in time-out each time he repeats the misbehavior. Then, you let him return to the center of household activity without further nagging.

The advantages of time-out are that you are communicating to your grandchild both verbally and nonverbally (by physically interrupting the misbehavior). Small children garner more from actions, than from words. Because the verbal disapproval is brief, you are not giving the misbehavior undue attention. You and your grandchild both have a chance to cool off before angry words or physical aggressions erupt. Your grandchild has a chance to contemplate his actions. Lastly, time-out is effective.

Temper Tantrums

A particular variety of disagreeable behavior, the temper tantrum, deserves special consideration. You do remember this type of behavior? To refresh your memory, imagine that you are in the grocery store. Your child wants to open the box of chocolate cake (which you intended to serve at your dinner party) in the shopping cart and eat it on the spot. You say No! and your little angel lies down on the floor and kicks and screams while other shoppers cast disdainful looks your way.

Most children have at least a few of these fits between the ages of one and three. Many parents and grandparents react to a child's temper tantrums with shame, embarrassment, and irritation at not being able to control the child. Children caught in the throes of a tantrum don't seem to be enjoying themselves either.

So, why do children throw these awful fits? Think about life from a small child's point of view. Big people are constantly ordering you around. The more tired and hungry you are, the harder it is to take. Besides, you have been working since birth to be like those big people and still lack competency in so many things. So you see, the key elements that act like tinder and a match to ignite a temper tantrum are fatigue, hunger, and frustration.

Please don't blame the parents if your grandchild has temper tantrums. Temper tantrums are a normal phase of child development. Children are learning about expressing negative emotions. Unfortunately, they often can't partition emotional responses from physical reactions. If a small child is happy, she skips and claps her hands. If she is miserable, she falls down on the floor and wails. Over time, children learn to express their feelings in more acceptable ways.

What can you do to avoid these ugly scenes? Anticipation and avoidance are important, because it is virtually impossible to stop a tantrum after it begins. If you are taking care of your grandchild, provide some unstructured time during the day when your grandchild can play without your frequent interference. If your home is child proofed, you will encounter fewer situations that force you to make rules or prompt you to shriek, "NO, don't touch that!"

Furthermore, you can reduce your grandchild's level of frustration at being so powerless by giving him choices (but not too many as to be overwhelming and confusing). For example, when your grandson refuses to climb into his car-seat, calmly ask, "Would you like to get in your car-seat by yourself, or would you like me to put you in?"

What can you do to prepare yourself should your grandchild someday throw a tantrum? First of all, consider what rules and limits the parents have established. Your grandson may be angry if you refuse to allow him to watch "Sesame Street" on television when his parents always permit this luxury. Next, find out in advance how the parents deal with tantrums.

Most experts recommend one of three strategies. One notion is that a child having a tantrum feels overwhelmed by his own anger and is frightened to be so totally out of control. According to strategy number one, you can help your flailing grandchild by comforting him. You pick him up, hold him close, and speak to him in soothing tones. However, if involving yourself with your grandchild causes *you* to become angry and emotionally out of control, or the tantrum is attention seeking in nature, you will only fuel the tantrum.

Alternatively, you ignore the tantrum. In other words you either walk away or put your grandchild in a quiet place where he can be alone until the storm subsides. After he quiets, you can go to your grandchild to comfort him and calmly discuss what happened. Never do you want to reinforce this sort of unattractive behavior by giving in to your grandchild's whims.

Thirdly, if your grandchild is doing something intolerable during the tantrum (hurting someone, breaking something, whining, hanging on your leg), then you can use time-out. (See previous section for how to employ time-out.)

What you don't want to do is to reinforce the recurrence of the tantrum by giving in to your grandchild's demands. This principle is true for most misbehaviors.

That doesn't mean that you must be totally unsympathetic to your grandchild's point of view. You can stand firm in your decision while still showing some understanding. Don't deny your grandchild's feelings. Rather, help him to identify these negative emotions. For example, "I know you are angry because I won't let you watch the *Texas Chain Saw Massacre*, but I won't abide this variety of television viewing in my home." After your grandchild has regained control of himself, don't nag at him. Start over with a clean slate and make him feel that you still accept and love him.

Sleeping Through the Night

As part of the old view of newborns as manipulative creatures, some parents were encouraged to start training their babies to sleep through the night from day one by refusing to feed them in the wee hours and instead leaving them to "cry it out." Now, it is recognized that most newborns cannot go more than three or four hours without becoming ravenously hungry. Because breast milk is so readily digested, breast-fed babies sometimes cannot even go that long. Because infants are growing rapidly (including their brains), they deserve the calories.

The age at which babies can sleep through the night varies. Some infants begin to sleep eight continuous hours during their

167

second month of life. The dogma has been that, by four months of age, 95 percent of babies can skip the middle-of-the-night feeding.

More recently, a study on infant sleep behavior concluded that although this standard holds true for bottle-fed babies, breast-fed babies have entirely different sleep/wake patterns. They tend to sleep less and for shorter intervals. Some breast-fed babies may not sleep through the night until weaned from the breast. (Perhaps it would be best if you shielded your weary children from this interesting academic tidbit. Otherwise, you might discover your grandbaby on your doorstep with a note pinned to his sleeper explaining that his parents have hastily departed for darkest Africa.)

Babies can fall into poor sleep habits. One of the most common stumbling blocks is failing to put a baby to bed while she is still awake. If your grandbaby becomes reliant upon a bridge to sleep (being nursed, bottle-fed, rocked), she may be unable to fall back to sleep without one of these crutches when she awakens during the night. (Most humans, whether they are aware of it or not, awaken intermittently during the night.)

Be aware that one remedy for breaking a child's habit of middle-of-the-night awakening is to send said child to the grandparents for a night or two. Generally, a child will not cry persistently if she knows those suckers, Mommy and Daddy, are not around.

A complete discussion of the many variations of childhood sleep disorders is beyond the scope of this book. Most bookstores have publications addressing the subject in depth.

Pacifiers and Thumb-Sucking

During the first three months of life most babies have an intense need to suck, which goes beyond the stimulation they receive during feedings from bottle or breast. Many breast-fed babies are able to satisfy this need by continued suckling at the breast after the meal is over. Otherwise, the usual outlets available to most babies are their own fingers or thumb or the pacifier. (Barring the above, babies have been known to resort to Grampa's nose or Gramma's spectacles.)

A generation ago, pacifiers were considered taboo. Critics objected to pacifiers on the grounds that the devises made a baby look silly, deformed teeth, and destroyed moral fiber. Although silliness is the eye of the beholder, the latter two accusations are unfounded.

The 1985 edition of Dr. Spock's Baby and Child Care offers a very sensible discussion on this subject. If given the pacifier very early, before thumb sucking becomes a habit, most babies are ready to give it up between three and six months when the urge to suck greatly diminishes. Admittedly, some babies, especially those whose parents became dependent upon offering the pacifier as a solution for Junior's every whimper, may continue to use the pacifier until they are one to two years old.

On the other hand, many infants who take up thumb sucking in lieu of a pacifier refuse to give up their thumb as a means of comforting themselves until they are three to five years old. It seems that the thumb is a more "precious comforter"—meaning it satisfies more than the need to suck. Furthermore, you can't take the thumb away or control how often it goes in a child's mouth.

If the parents elect to give your grandbaby a pacifier, try to go along with their decision. (Some advice on safety—do not tie a loop of string or ribbon around the pacifier; it might become tangled around her little neck.)

Independence

At birth, your grandbaby has no idea who she is, where her body ends, or how she is distinct from you when you cuddle her. Around six months of age, your grandbaby begins to grasp the astonishing concept of her self as separate from her loved ones. Coincidentally, she begins to learn to do a few simple things by herself. For instance, she may push away your hands if you try to hold the bottle, preferring to manage it herself. Thus starts the long trek along the path toward independence.

By the end of the first year, the battle for independence intensifies. Child development experts love to comment about the paradoxical simultaneous increase in independence and dependence at this age. It is as though a baby's increased ability to do things like walk (which can move her away as well as toward loved ones) is both exciting and frightening.

One of the greatest services parents and grandparents can do for children is to help them become independent, secure, and happy adults. If you agree that independence is truly a desirable trait, how can you encourage self-sufficiency in your grandchild? By providing your grandchild with security, love, and reassurance without smothering her, and by giving your grandchild the freedom to explore her environment and test her skills while you observe from the wings.

Sometimes you may have to fight your inclinations to maintain order and cleanliness for the sake of encouraging independence in your grandchild. A walk with your toddling grandchild is brisker and less random if he rides in the stroller. A mealtime is tidier if you feed your grandbaby yourself. Your grandchild's clothes stay cleaner if you forbid him to play in the garden. Nevertheless, if you encourage your grandchild to explore and to do things himself (when such behavior is developmentally appropriate), you are helping him to master valuable skills. And, when your grandchild accomplishes a task, no matter how small it might seem to you, he gains self-confidence.

Toilet Training

The attitude toward toilet training at the beginning of the twentieth century was one of permissiveness. Rigidity set in during the mid-1930s as parents adopted strict timetables, structured schedules, and coercive methods to potty train their infants as early as possible. Many of these children grew up to meet Freud's description of the anal-compulsive personality.

Leniency with regard to toilet training is back in vogue, to the extent that you may ask yourself, "Are those parents *ever* going to toilet train my grandchild?"

Why are parents tending to postpone toilet training their children compared to your generation? First and foremost, training a very young child requires too much effort. As a child gets old enough to follow simple directions and understand key words like "wet," "dry," "pee," "poop," to control bladder and bowel reflexes, to walk to the toilet and pull down (and then up) his pants..., he becomes very easy to toilet train. Parents or grandparents who attempt to toilet train a baby lacking these skills, are really training themselves to catch baby's bodily fluids and solids. And, if these adults communicate disappointment to the baby for his "accidents," they risk making this youngster feel guilty and incompetent.

Most child experts recommend waiting until a toddler is at least two years old before starting potty training. The signs that the child is ready include her asking to be changed when the diaper is wet or dirty and communicating an awareness of impending urination and defecation. The surest sign is when the child insists, "I don't want to wear a diaper. I want to use the potty." If you wait long enough, a child will train herself.

In order to be considered truly toilet trained, a child must be able to go to the bathroom without reminder and use the toilet without any assistance or supervision. Many children are not capable of *independent* toileting until they are three years old. Even at that age, only 66 percent of children have achieved nighttime dryness.

So, the message here is that if your grandchild is not toilet trained (and especially if he is under three years of age), don't worry about it. Don't pester the parents, saying things like, "Is Junior *still* in diapers?" Don't make your grandchild feel remiss. Most normal children are out of diapers by the time they enter school.

There you have it—the tip of the child-behavior iceberg. If you find the subject fascinating and hunger for more information, check the recommended reading list in the appendix.

Chapter Thirteen

GUESS WHO'S COMING TO VISIT?

You grandparents ought to be advised of a recent survey in which parents were asked, "In whose care would you prefer to leave your children?" Ninety-nine percent of these parents answered, "Their grandparents." The next popular choice was a middle-aged nun. Although this enormous trust in your child rearing skills is flattering, it can also become overwhelming.

Imagine that your daughter proudly announces she is expecting number six. One solution is to make yourself less available as a sitter by retiring to a remote locale. We suggest that you avoid vacation resorts. Rather, choose a spot where your children are unlikely to visit. This eliminates the East Coast, the West Coast, the Rocky Mountains, the Caribbean, and Western Europe.

A less-drastic solution to being overly popular as a baby-sitter is simply to tell the parents how much and how often you would be willing to watch your grandchildren. Hopefully, they will understand that you already had the enriching experience of being a parent.

174

You are in the enviable position of being able to play with your adorable grandchildren in small doses. You come to the arena of child care armed with your past experiences and with the enthusiasm that comes from *not* being with the children twenty hours a day, seven days a week. You can defer the role of gatekeeper and rule maker to the parents and adopt the infinitely more enjoyable role of playmate instead.

You will be faced with basically two baby-sitting situations: you will go to the home of your grandchildren or they will come to yours. The advantages of the former are that all of the child-care essentials are presumably there already, the child is in familiar surroundings, and your property is not at risk for demolition. The advantages of the latter are that you are on your own turf and the child has the stimulation of exploring a new environment.

This chapter was written to provide you with guidelines for grandbaby-sitting. You needn't feel compelled to strictly follow every helpful hint (especially the facetious ones), nor to rush out and procure everything on the essential items list. If your grandchild is coming to your home, you can go over the list with the parents to find out what things they plan to supply. Normally, the parents will bring clothes, pacifiers, bottles, special medicines, favorite toys and "security blankets." They may also want to supply things like strollers and car-seats. If you need to supply some items, ask the parents about preferred product brands. (For more information on buying for baby, see Chapter three.)

Essential Items to Have on Hand When Grandbaby Comes to Visit:

Day-to-Day
> diapers
> diaper wipes
> diaper pail
> bottles
> bottle brush
> age-appropriate feeding implements
>> (small teaspoon, trainer cup, bowl, plate, bib)

formula or expressed breast milk
for older baby or child: low-fat milk, juice, cereals,
  and appropriate solids (ask parents about diet)
clothes, including weather-appropriate outdoor garments
  and hats for warmth or sun protection

Transportation
  car-seat
  for walks, one of the following: stroller, backpack,
    front carrier, wagon

Toiletries
  baby shampoo
  mild soap
  mild lotion
  ointment for diaper area (Desitin, petroleum jelly,
    A & D...)
  scissors with small rounded ends, nail clippers, or file

Toys
  simple and versatile: balls, hand games, plastic cooking
    utensils and containers, mirrors, music, magazines and
    books, etc.
  You can rent, borrow, make, or buy used or new toys.
  Parents should bring favorite cuddlies.

Medical Supplies
  acetaminophen (Tylenol, Tempra, Panadol, Liquiprin), syrup
    of ipecac
  sunblock (PABA-free for small infants)
  thermometer (rectal)
  first aid: bandages, gauze, cotton, rubbing alcohol, hydrogen
    peroxide, antibacterial ointment, prescription medications,
    vitamins

Furniture
  a safe place for baby to sleep (crib, playpen)
  a safe place for baby to sit if unable to sit unassisted
    (infant seat, bouncy chair)

Helpful Hints to Prepare for a Grandbaby-sitting Session

☐ Make sure you have a list of important phone numbers: the parents, poison control, the pediatrician, the ambulance, your psychiatrist.... If your grandchild is coming to your home and you live in a different town, get the name of a family doctor or pediatrician.

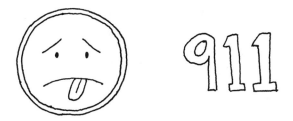

☐ Child proof your home. For the most part, your common sense will guide you in moving potentially harmful things out of your granchildren's reach. Basically, you want to protect tiny people from objects that are breakable, sharp, hot, electrical in nature, toxic (cleaning agents, many cosmetics, solvents, all medications), small enough to fit inside tiny mouths (but not nutritious), steep (stairs), and very wet (pools, ponds, tubs). Also, you will want to protect your valuables from exploring fingers.

☐ Ask the parents about the Routine. Knowing all those wonderful mundane details of your grandchild's day-to-day life is the secret to a smooth transition when you take the reins. You will help make Junior comfortable by following the customary schedules and rules. Don't blatantly ignore rules that the parents have established about things such as foods, bedtimes, and television watching. At least, don't brag about such breaches to the parents.

177

☐ Equip your home for your grandchild's visit (see table on Essential Items...). This shouldn't push you into bankruptcy. Almost anything (other than perishable goods) can be purchased second hand, rented, or borrowed. For instance, rather than buy a shelf full of children's classics, you might check out books from the public library.

☐ Review all those wonderful nursery rhymes, songs, and stories. Have you ever really paid attention to the subject matter of these traditional favorites? They deal with cheery subjects like spiders frightening little girls, humanoid people falling off walls and fracturing their skulls, babies falling out of tree tops, husbands who keep their brides in pumpkin shells. No wonder children begin to have nightmares at such tender ages!

☐ Acquaint yourself with the array of delightful children's television programs such as "Sesame Street" and "Mr. Rogers' Neighborhood," videotapes, cassette tapes, and records. They may come in handy when you need a respite from entertaining your grandchild. (Bear in mind that most experts recommend that caretakers restrict the amount of time children watch television.)

☐ Purchase industrial-strength cleaning agents guaranteed to remove crayon and ink marks, petrified oatmeal, grape jam, and the like from walls, carpets, and upholstery. Hide said agents from Junior before he tries to drink them.

☐ Practice walking while looking down, and label miniature cars and trikes with day-glow stickers so you can dodge them when you go running to the nursery in the dark.

Child Proofing Your Home

LIVING ROOM

BREAKABLES, HEIRLOOMS, PRECIOUS PICTURES

VALUABLES

PROTECTIVE COVERING

PICASSO

BE CAUTIOUS OF FURNITURE W/TH SHARP CORNERS

WATCH OUT FOR THROW RUGS

SMALL OBJECTS CIG BUTS

* IF YOU DON'T WANT IT EATEN, BROKEN, CRAYONED, SPILLED ON, OR WET ON....... MOVE IT or PROTECT IT!

KITCHEN

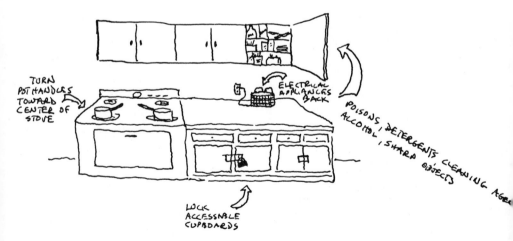

TURN POT HANDLES TOWARD CENTER OF STOVE

ELECTRICAL APPLIANCES BACK

POISONS, DETERGENTS, ALCOHOL, SHARP OBJECTS CLEANING AGENTS

LOCK ACCESSIBLE CUPBOARDS

BATHROOM

MAKE SURE ALL MEDICATIONS, VITAMINS, ASPIRIN, HAIRSPRAY & COSMETICS ARE OUT OF REACH

KEEP TOILET SEAT DOWN

NO WATER IN TUB

BEDROOM

FRAGILE & SHARP OBJECTS HAND MIRRORS

REMOVE MEDICINES HAIRPINS FROM NIGHTSTAND

LAUNDRY ROOM

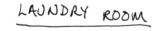

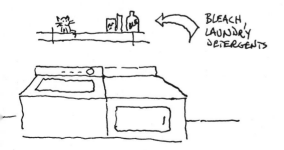

BLEACH, LAUNDRY DETERGENTS

181

STAIRS

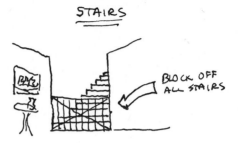

BLOCK OFF
ALL STAIRS

USE OUTLET CAPS

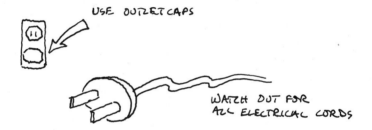

WATCH OUT FOR
ALL ELECTRICAL CORDS

HIGH PLACES

WHEN JUNIOR STARTS
CLIMBING, YOU CANNOT
LET HIM OUT OF YOUR
SIGHT!

MALL OBJECTS & SHARP OBJECTS

BUTTONS

HAIRPINS

TACKS & NAILS

PENCILS LETTER
OPENER'S.

KNITTING NEEDLES

LOOSE BUTTON EYES
ON TOYS

ANYTHING ON
STRINGS

HOT OBJECTS

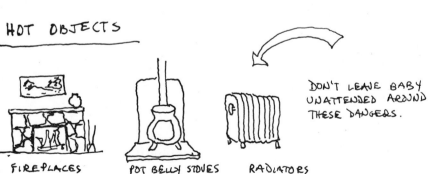

DON'T LEAVE BABY
UNATTENDED AROUND
THESE DANGERS.

FIREPLACES   POT BELLY STOVES   RADIATORS

183

What to Do if Your Grandbaby is Under the Weather

Hopefully your grandchildren are healthy and never fall ill under your care. Most babies are born healthy and live robust lives punctuated only by run-of-the-mill childhood illnesses. However, you just might happen to be the caretaker during one of those lapses of otherwise good health. If your grandchild is sick, you will, of course, want to contact the parents immediately. While you await their return from Bolivia, you can read the following review of the signs of illness in babies and the appropriate actions to take.

First of all, how do you know when a baby is not feeling well? If an older baby or child is really sick, her distress will be obvious even to the neophyte. During your stint as a parent, you probably learned to identify the onset of illness in your children by the way they looked: a certain glazing of the eyes, flushed cheeks or pallor, crabby or listless behavior. Simply "not looking or acting well" is often a reliable sign of impending illness.

Although a sick child is easy to spot, illness can manifest itself more subtly in the newly born. Your grandbaby cannot tell you what is the matter, leaving you to decide whether she is suffering from fatigue, gas, ear infection.... Furthermore, some indications of illness in older children (e.g., fever) are not reliable in babies.

Signs of Illness in Babies:

☐ Extreme irritability: the baby cannot be comforted or consoled.

☐ Extreme lethargy: the baby lies there listlessly (even while you take the temperature rectally).

☐ An unusual cry: the cry is higher pitched than normal or has a shrieking quality as though motivated by pain.

☐ Poor feeding: the baby either refuses to eat or has difficulty sucking or swallowing.

184

☐ Respiratory distress: the baby is breathing faster than normally, is breathing laboriously (the nostrils flare, the skin retracts between the ribs and above the collar bone with each breath), has a barking cough, and/or is making unusual noises when she breathes (harsh, crouping sounds when inhaling or wheezing sounds primarily with exhaling).

☐ A bluish tint to the lips, around the mouth and nail beds (cyanosis). Cyanosis indicates that something is wrong with the lungs or the heart.

☐ Jaundice or a yellowish cast to the skin and the whites of the eyes. (See Chapter nine.) Jaundice appearing after the first few weeks of life is cause for physician consultation.

☐ Repeated vomiting. This doesn't mean frequent "spitting up" of a small volume of stomach contents. (Until the ring of muscle between the esophagus and stomach matures, babies commonly spit up after meals.) Vomiting refers to a forceful regurgitation of a significant amount of partially digested food. A rather worrisome type of vomiting is called "projectile vomiting," when the vomitus follows an impressive trajectory and hits the wall three feet away.

☐ Diarrhea. This does not necessarily mean loose stools. A normal breast-fed baby's poops are usually frequent, yellowish, and unformed. If your grandbaby's stools have a ring of water around them, increase dramatically in frequency, and/or are accompanied by mucus, pus or blood, call the doctor.

☐ Evidence of dehydration. This condition occurs when a baby 1) has lost fluid in vomit or diarrhea, 2) has bled internally or externally, or 3) has been unable to drink sufficient fluids. Signs of dehydration include decreased urine output, dry skin, sunken eyes, depressed soft spot on top of the head (fontannel), lethargy, and decreased appetite.

185

- Seizures or convulsions. Babies don't always manifest seizure activity in the way adults do. They may have repetitive jerky movements of one or more extremities, merely stiffen, roll their eyes to one side, or cease to breathe for an abnormally long time.

- Choking. The baby may not be sick, but may have swallowed a foreign object or sucked material into his lung.

- Low or elevated body temperature.

More on Fever or the Lack Thereof

- What should a person's body temperature be? Most humans have an average body temperature of 98.6 degrees Fahrenheit as measured orally. A rectal temperature is usually one degree higher and an axillary (armpit) temperature is one degree lower. Body temperature varies a little depending upon the time of the day, activity level, one's state of dress or undress, and the weather.

- What is a fever? Fever is defined as an oral temperature of more than 100 degrees Fahrenheit or a rectal temperature of more than 100.4. If the temperature is between 100 and 101, it should be taken again in an hour before calling it a fever.

- How does one take a baby's temperature? The easiest way is to politely ask someone else, a paid professional for instance, to do it for you. Unfortunately, when you phone for advice, one of the first things the doctor or nurse will ask you is, "What is the baby's temperature?"

- It is not a good idea to place the thermometer in your grandbaby's mouth and expect her to cooperatively hold it there without trying to eat the thing. It is better to employ the axillary or the rectal method.

- Most doctors recommend using a standard glass mercury thermometer. It is inexpensive and accurate. Unless you can afford the type of digital thermometer used by hospitals (and are willing to calibrate it at intervals), this type of thermometer can display erratic readings. The "sensor strips" that are taped on a child's forehead are often inaccurate.

☐ To take a rectal temperature, shake the thermometer down and lubricate the correct end with a lubricating gel (e.g., petroleum jelly). After spreading the buttocks of your prone grandbaby, grasp the thermometer one inch from the bottom and gently insert that one inch into her rectum. Then, pinch your squirming grandbaby's buttocks tightly together, and hold the thermometer in place for two to three minutes.

☐ To take an axillary temperature, shake the thermometer own and place the bulb in your grandbaby's armpit. Hold her arm snugly against her chest for about five minutes.

☐ What is the significance of a fever? Babies and toddlers don't respond to illness with elevations in body temperature the way adults do. Babies can be very ill with a subnormal or even a normal temperature. Toddlers can mount a relatively high fever with a mere runny nose.
The key is how the baby or child is acting. Older babies and toddlers who are feverish but who aren't acting lethargic or excessively irritable, vomiting, refusing fluids, or having convulsions are usually not of concern.
Are fevers harmful? In general, the cause of the fever (bacteria, viruses, etc.), rather than the fever itself, is what is harmful. Fever doesn't cause brain damage until the temperature reaches 107 or 108 degrees Fahrenheit. Fortunately, the brain's regulatory mechanisms usually keeps fevers below 104.

☐ Actually, elevated body temperature is one way the body defends itself from infection. Fever makes the white blood cells of the immune system move faster, the better to destroy bacteria. Also, elevated temperature stimulates the body's production of interferon, a substance that inhibits viral replication.

☐ When should you call the doctor if the temperature is abnormal? Any baby less than two months of age with a fever should be seen by a doctor. For babies between two and six months of age, a doctor should be called if the temperature is more than 101 degrees Fahrenheit. For an older child, call a physician for temperatures greater than 103 or temperatures of 101 for more than 48 hours. Always call the doctor when a child is acting very sick.

☐ When should you treat a fever? Check with the physician. Usually, the philosophy is to treat fevers of over 102 degrees Fahrenheit, and then only if the child is uncomfortable. If your grandchild has a history of seizures precipitated by fever, consult the doctor.

☐ How do you treat a fever? Remove excess clothing, discourage vigorous activity, and encourage fluids. The fever-reducing medication of choice for children over two months of age is acetaminophen (Tylenol, Tempra, Panadol, Liquiprin). It comes in drops for infants, and elixir and chewable tablets for older children. The dose is based on body weight. A dosage chart should be included with the medication. If you are uncertain about the correct dose, call the physician.

☐ What about aspirin? Reye syndrome has been linked to aspirin use in children suffering from viral infections. Reye syndrome is characterized by high fever, vomiting, and combative behavior which can progress to convulsions, coma, and death. Many pediatricians have stopped recommending aspirin for fevers associated with most illness.

☐ What about sponging? Many authorities discourage sponging on the basis that it does not effectively reduce fever and that it often makes a fussy child more fretful and uncomfortable.

When to Call A Physician

☐ Your grandbaby is exhibiting signs of illness such as irritability, lethargy, unusual cry, poor feeding, respiratory distress, cyanosis, jaundice, vomiting, diarrhea, dehydration, seizures, fever.

☐ Your grandbaby looks and acts sick.

☐ Cardiopulmonary arrest (no breathing, no heartbeat, or both).

☐ Aspiration, meaning a baby puts something in her mouth and it goes "down the wrong way" into her lungs causing choking or respiratory distress.

☐ Trauma such as a head injury, laceration (cut), burn, electrical shock, and so on.

☐ Accidental ingestion: medications, alcohol, cleaning agents, gasoline, plants that may be poisonous, batteries, and other small objects. If you have a Poison Control Center in your area, call them first. An expert should be able to tell you whether the substance is indeed dangerous in the amount ingested and what steps you should take. Have syrup of ipecac on hand in the event that you are advised to immediately induce vomiting.

☐ In order to quickly handle medical emergencies, keep emergency phone numbers handy (physician, hospital, poison control, 911), know basic first aid, and learn how to do CPR (cardiopulmonary resuscitation). Basic first aid training and the elements of CPR are beyond the scope of this book. Most communities offer classes, and local bookstores and libraries have appropriate reading materials.

Things the Doctor Will Want to Know When You Telephone:

☐ your grandchild's name

☐ her age

☐ her baseline state of health (Does she have an underlying chronic illness or is she usually healthy?)

☐ when the child began to act sick, how long has she continued to be ill

☐ If you have given acetaminophen, tell the doctor when the last dose was given and whether it helped reduce fever.

☐ If your grandbaby is not keeping down fluids or if she seems to be making less wet diapers, be specific about the number of ounces she drank and the number of wet diapers produced within a period of time.

The Grandparent Book has provided you with a lot of information on pregnancy, prenatal care, childbirth, child development, child care, child behavior, and infant illness. The objective was twofold: 1) to help you understand the parents' perspective, because understanding is the basis of a good relationship; and 2) to review any infant-care basics you may have forgotten, because preparation fosters self-confidence.

Did you *really* need to know any of this information? No, not really. Being an *informed* grandparent may help you avoid conflict with the parents, but it isn't critical to being a *wonderful* grandparent.

What will make you a wonderful grandparent? Love. All you really need to do is love your grandchildren and your children. Love them openly. Don't keep it to yourself. Make each person feel your love.

A grandchild will know he is loved if you always treat him with kindness and respect, if you avoid judging him and comparing him to others, if you express joy at his achievements (no matter how small), if you find time to really *be* with him.

Why is your focused, unconditional love so important? Because when you love someone, you nurture the sense of self-worth. By building your grandchild's self-esteem, you have given her the foundation for success. She is more likely to be physically healthy, to have friends, to excel academically, to be creative, to be a leader. If you have faith in your grandchild, she will come to have faith in herself.

Also, when you love someone, it makes *you* feel good. When you love freely, the emotion is usually mirrored. It feels good to be loved, too.

Along with parents, teachers, and friends, you can play an important role in making your grandchildren feel valued. Your love is powerful. Share it!

APPENDIX

GLOSSARY

abruptio placenta - premature separation of the placenta from the uterine wall, a cause of third trimester bleeding and pain.

alpha fetoprotein - a chemical released in higher than normal levels in fetuses with neural tube defects, which can be detected in the mother's blood.

amniocentesis - a prenatal diagnostic test in which a small amount of amniotic fluid is withdrawn to test the fetus for a variety of hereditary disorders.

amniotic fluid - the watery substance within the "bag of waters," which surrounds and protects the fetus.

breech - emergence of the baby's buttocks or feet first during labor as opposed to the normal emergence of head first.

cervix - the "neck" of the uterus containing a hole or "os," which dilates during labor to allow your grandbaby to pass from the uterus to the vagina.

Cesarean section - delivering the baby surgically by cutting through the mother's abdominal wall and uterus.

circumcision - removal of the prepuce, or foreskin, of the penis.

echosonography - a diagnostic procedure using high-frequency sound waves to produce images of various internal organs. It is used prenatally to visualize the developing fetus and in the form of a Doptone to listen to the fetal heart sounds.

ectopic pregnancy - a pregnancy in which the fertilized egg implants somewhere other than the uterus, e.g., the Fallopian tube, ovary, abdomen, etc.

embryo - the technical name for your future grandbaby between two weeks after fertilization (before which time he/she is called a **zygote**) until the end of the seventh or eighth week of gestation.

epidural anesthesia - a method of numbing pain in which an anesthetic is injected in the low back just outside the membranes surrounding the spinal cord.

episiotomy - a surgical incision enlarging the opening of the vagina to facilitate birth.

estimated date of confinement or E.D.C. - the approximate date that your grandbaby should make her debut, called the "due date."

Fallopian tubes - the conduits between the ovaries and the uterus.

fetus - the technical name for your future grandbaby between the time when major structures have been outlined (about the eighth week of gestation) and birth.

fertilization - the fusion of the ovum or egg from the mother with one sperm from the father; conception.

forceps - an instrument with two blades and a handle about the size of salad spoons used to grasp the baby's head if the mother is unable to push the baby out during delivery. Vacuum extraction forceps have a suction cup which fits on the baby's head.

gametes - sperm and ova, the elements of reproduction.

gestation - pregnancy; the time between conception and birth.

human chorionic gonadotrophin or HCG - a hormone made by the placenta during early pregnancy. It is the chemical detected by pregnancy tests.

in vitro fertilization - the fertilization of the ova by the sperm takes place outside the body (in a laboratory dish). The embryo is subsequently transferred to the uterus.

meconium - the sticky, green-black stool produced by the newborn for the first day or two of life.

neonatologist - a physician specializing in newborn care.

neural tube defect - a type of birth disorder in which the brain and/or spinal cord does not develop properly.

obstetrician - a physician specializing in the management of pregnancy and birth.

ovary - the female gonad; produces ova. (?omit?)

ovum (ova, plural) - egg produced by the ovary.

perinatologist - a physician with specialized training in the period shortly before and after birth.

placenta - an organ within the mother's uterus that allows an exchange of nutrients and wastes between your grandbaby-to-be and his mother.

placenta previa - a condition in which the placenta is situated abnormally low in the uterus, such that it partly or completely blocks the cervix.

postpartum or post partum - subsequent to childbirth.

prenatal - before birth.

sonography - see echosonography

term - the culmination of the nine months of pregnancy. A "term" baby is one delivered when expected, rather than too early (prematurely) or too late (postmaturely).

trimester - a period of three months. The nine months of pregnancy are divided into three trimesters.

ultrasound - see echosonography.

umbilical cord - the link between your grandbaby-to-be and the placenta.

uterus - womb.

vagina - birth canal.

RECOMMENDED READING

PREGNANCY

The Complete Books of Pregnancy and Childbirth, Sheila Kitzinger, Alfred A. Knopf, 1982.

Complete Pregnancy & Baby Book, Vicky Lansky and Consumer Guide Editors, Publications International, 1987.

The Well Pregnancy Book, Mike Samuels, M.D. & Nancy Samuels, Summit Books, 1986.

BABY AND CHILD CARE

Your Baby and Child, Penelope Leach, Alfred A. Knopf Publishers, 1978.

Dr. Mom, Marianne Neifert, M.D., Signet Books, 1986.

The Well Baby Book and *The Well Child Book*, Mike Samuels, M.D. and Nancy Samuels, Summit Books.

Your Child's Health, Barton D. Schmitt, M.D., Bantam Books, 1987.

Dr. Spock's Baby and Child Care, Benjamin Spock, M.D. & Michael B. Rothenberg, M.D., Simon & Schuster, 1985.

Redirecting Children's Misbehavior, Kvols-Riedler, Bill & Kathy, Rdic Publications, 1979.

CHILD DEVELOPMENT

Any books by T. Berry Brazleton.

The First Twelve Months of Life and *The Second Twelve Months of Life*, Frank Caplan, Perigee Books.

The Magic Years, Selma Fraiberg, Scribners, 1968.

Books by the Gesell Institute.

GRANDPARENTING

Congratulations! You're Going to be a Grandmother, Lanie Carter, Oak Tree, 1980.

The New American Grandparent, a sociological study by Andrew Cherlin and Frand Furstenberg, Basic Books, 1986.

How to Grandparent, Fitzhugh Dodson, Harper and Row, 1981.

A Book for Grandmothers, Ruth Goode, Macmillan, 1976.

The Grandparents' Handbook, Hugh Jolly, Pagoda Books, 1984.

Grandparents and Grandchildren: The Vital Connection, Arthur Kornhaber, Anchor Press/Doubleday, 1981.

Between Parents and Grandparents, Arthur Kornhaber, St. Martin's Press, 1986.

Index